Rhythms of Religious Ritual

The Yearly Cycles of
Jews, Christians, and Muslims

Rhythms of Religious Ritual

The Yearly Cycles of Jews, Christians, and Muslims

Kathy Black

with Bishop Kyrillos,
Jonathan L. Friedmann and Tamar Frankiel,
Hamid Mavani and Jihad Turk

CLAREMONT STUDIES IN
INTERRELIGIOUS DIALOGUE 1

Rhythms of Religious Ritual
The Yearly Cycles of Jews, Christians, and Muslims

©2018 Claremont Press
1325 N. College Ave
Claremont, CA 91711

ISBN 978-1-946230-15-7

Library of Congress Cataloging-in-Publication Data

Religious Ritual
The Yearly Cycles of Jews, Christians, and Muslims / Kathy
Black with Bishop Kyrillos, Jonathan L. Friedmann, Tamar
Frankiel, Hamid Mavani and Jihad Turk
       viii + 157 pp. 22 x 15 cm. –(Claremont Studies in
       Interreligious Dialogue)
       ISBN 978-1-946230-15-7
       1. Judaism, Liturgy, 21st century
       2. Liturgics
       3. Rites and ceremonies, United States, Judaism,
          Christianity, Islam
       BM660 B53 2018

Table of Contents

Preface

The idea for this book came from colleagues and students affiliated with an interreligious experiment which has become a rich new partnership between the Claremont School of Theology (CST – a Christian graduate institution, mostly Protestant in affiliation), The Academy of Jewish Religion, California (AJR/CA – a Jewish seminary), Bayan Claremont (Bayan – a new Islamic graduate institution), and the University of the West (UWest – a Buddhist educational institution). Located on CST's campus is also the Saint Athanasius and Saint Cyril Theological School (ACTS – a Coptic Orthodox Christian seminary).[1]

Having colleagues in worship/prayer and preaching in these other religious traditions makes for rich dialogue, sparks the imagination and raises curiosity about religious practices as well as beliefs. Having students on campus who are practitioners as well as students interested in the academic understanding of these various religions causes us to be acutely aware of the various rhythms of ritual practice – high holy days of celebration and those of repentance and self-examination, days of feasting and fasting. Formed by the yearly ritual calendar of my own Christian Protestant tradition, I set out on a journey to learn about and document the yearly ritual calendars of the siblings of faith: Judaism and Islam. Once written, I recruited colleagues from AJR/CA and Bayan to assist me in this project and I am deeply indebted to all of them for their additions, corrections, and editing skills – especially to Jonathan

---

[1] At the initial writing of this book, CST also had a Center for South Asian Religions (Hinduism, Jainism, and Buddhism).

Friedmann whose wise counsel and critical eye has been invaluable throughout this process.

Our hope is that in addition to learning about the history and beliefs of other religious traditions, students of religion and religious practitioners will also learn about the yearly practices and rhythms of religious ritual that form communities of faith.

Kathy Black
Claremont, CA
2018

Contributors

Rev. Dr. Kathy Black is an ordained minister of the United Methodist denomination of the Protestant branch of Christianity and is the Gerald Kennedy Chair of Homiletics and Liturgics at the Claremont School of Theology, Claremont, CA. She has published in the field of multicultural Christian worship.

Tamar Frankiel, PhD is Professor of Comparative Religion at the Academy for Jewish Religion, California, (AJR/CA) where she teaches liturgy, world religions, and modern Jewish history. She previously has served AJR/CA as Dean of Academic Affairs, Provost, and President. An observant Jew, she has published numerous books in American religious history, and in Jewish spirituality and mysticism.

Jonathan L. Friedmann is a cantor, composer, biblical scholar, and musicologist. He is also Professor of Jewish Music History at the Academy for Jewish Religion California, Extraordinary Associate Professor of Theology at North-West University, Potchefstroom, South Africa (NWU), and a Research Fellow at NWU in Musical Arts in South Africa: Resources and Applications. He is involved in Humanistic Judaism.

Bishop Kyrillos is an auxiliary bishop in the Diocese of Los Angeles, Southern California and Hawaii of the Coptic Orthodox Church and Dean of St. Athanasius and St. Cyril Theological Coptic Orthodox Theological School in Claremont, CA.

Hamid Mavani is Associate Professor of Islamic Studies at Bayan Claremont, Claremont, CA. His expertise in Islamic Studies stems from both academic training at Universities as well as specialized theological training at the traditional seminaries in the Muslim world.

Jihad Turk is the founding president of Bayan Claremont, an Islamic graduate school designed to educate Muslim scholars and religious leaders. He previously served as the Imam/Director of Religious Affairs at the Islamic Center of Southern California, the oldest and largest mosque in the Los Angeles area.

Introduction

The world of the 21st century in North America is becoming increasingly populated by persons who adhere to a wide diversity of religious perspectives, including no religious beliefs at all. The notion that the United States of America is a Christian country cannot be sustained any longer, if it ever was true. We live in a multi-religious context while fewer and fewer persons practice any form of religion. Increasingly, immediate and extended families are comprised of persons with varying commitments to different religions. We also recognize that there are religious "hybrids" among us who are Christian/Buddhist or Jewish/Christian because of interreligious marriages or personal affiliations to more than one religious tradition.

As we navigate this multi-religious world, there are many "world religions" or "comparative religion" books written about the history, tenets, and sacred texts of many of the religions in the world – especially the three religions that have their roots in the historical figure of Abraham: Judaism, Christianity, and Islam. These are excellent resources in one's quest to understand the differences and similarities found among these three great religions. Focusing primarily on history, tenets, and texts however, these books can only give cursory attention to the broad "practices" engaged in by adherents of these three religions as they participate in the various occasions for ritual observance.

For practicing Jews, Christians or Muslims, however, it is often the rhythms of their yearly religious calendar that provide an underlying foundation for their lives – their thoughts, moods, emotions, self-assessments, actions, spiritual practices, engagement in prayer and communal participation in religious observances. For each religion, there are times during the religious year that are designed for inner reflection on one's spiritual life – a personal inventory of how one is making progress or missing the mark in adherence to their religious tradition. And there are times in the year when our religions call us to reach out to others in acts of kindness, justice, charity and mercy. This is not to say that both the inward life and outward expressions of one's religion are not a part of one's daily religious practice. It is to say however, that each religion sets aside times during the year when collectively the community pays a little more attention to one expression over the other.

The special ritual occasions that highlight the year within each religion have been formed by specific beliefs but are most notably rooted in a metanarrative, a story of grand proportions, that underlies the practices. The adherents to these three religious groups are "people of a book" – sacred text(s) that form the basis of the narratives. The yearly cycles of each religion retell key moments of the metanarrative, remember important events, and provide opportunities to reconnect to our roots in history.

The yearly cycle raises to the fore highlights of the metanarrative, the textual documents that support the narrative, the historical traditions, and the theological beliefs associated with each. As we participate in the observance of each of the ritual occasions in the cycle, we remember the stories of our faith and recommit our lives to following the teachings that are foundational to our respective religion. Throughout time, specific worship/prayer practices, symbols and/or symbolic gestures have become associated with many episodes in the narrative and each occasion that is observed in some fashion. Customs regarding what to eat, what to wear, and what to do have also emerged.

This book seeks to address the unique ways that each of these three religions retells/reenacts/remembers their metanarrative on a yearly basis through ritual gatherings known as festivals, seasons, holidays, holy days, "occasions". It is an attempt to identify the yearly rhythms that guide our common yearnings for religious ritual practice.

We recognize the sheer magnitude and complex nature (not to mention the ludicrous attempt) of such an undertaking because each of these religions has "branches" that have grown out of the original trunk of the tree. Judaism is historically divided between Ashkenazic and Sephardic, and Ashkenazic Judaism now has four major branches: Orthodox, Conservative, Reconstructionist, and Reform with diversity within each, along with minor branches such as Renewal, Humanistic, and Transdenominational. Christianity includes Orthodox Christianity, Roman Catholicism, and Protestantism (with two main branches within Orthodoxy and hundreds of denominations within Protestantism as well as offshoots that don't fit neatly into any of these categories).

Likewise, Muslims are not a monolithic group and exhibit great diversity within. They can be divided into two major groups: Sunnis and Shias. The former consists of four schools of thought (*madhabs*): Hanafi, Maliki, Shafi'i and Hanbali. The major branches amongst the Shias are: Twelvers, Isma'ilis, Zaydis, and Bohras with the overwhelming majority being Twelvers. The mystical tradition within Islam is expressed in Sufism. Both Sunnis and Shias have embraced aspects of the Sufi tradition to various degrees.

It is true that *intrafaith* beliefs and practices (those differences within a particular religion) are often as diverse

3

as *interfaith* beliefs and practices. Each denomination and subset has diverse opinions about the level of importance as well as the specific practices associated with each yearly observance. In some instances, the degree of importance and practices are denominationally rooted; in other instances, they are determined by the national or local cultures. The Islamic celebration of Eid al-Adha will take on different practices by African American Muslims who converted to Islam through the teachings and influence of Malcolm X than American Muslims who immigrated from Turkey or Iran. Or, the minor observance of Chanukah in Judaism will take on greater significance in the United States because it occurs at the same time as Christians are celebrating the birth of Jesus and therefore becomes an alternative for Jewish children to the parties and gift-giving of the North American Christian influenced culture.

Despite the great diversity present within each religion and the many limitations of such a project, for the most part, there is still a story, traditions and texts that guide these yearly cycles. It is the broad scope of these yearly religious/ritual/worship observances for each religion that we hope to highlight here.

The creation of an interfaith seminary collaborative in Southern California precipitated the idea for this book. Three graduate educational institutions initially partnered together so that students and faculty of all the institutions could learn more about one another, dispel stereotypes of the "other," and collaborate on issues related to the common good for our communities and peacemaking in our world: Claremont School of Theology (an ecumenical Christian seminary)[1], the Academy of Jewish Religion,

---

[1] Because the student population at Claremont School of Theology is primarily Protestant in orientation, and because this book was written with our collaborative context in mind (Claremont School of Theology, Bayan Claremont, and the Academy of Jewish Religion, California), the Christian chapter will most likely reveal a more Protestant slant.

California (an ecumenical Jewish seminary), and Bayan Claremont (a new ecumenical Islamic graduate institution).[1] Students have the opportunity to train in the same classroom for a wide variety of leadership roles within their respective religious communities (rabbis, ministers, imams, chaplains, teachers, scholars), in interfaith settings, non-profit organizations, and secular environments. Having practitioners of various religious traditions in the same classroom, participating in co-curricular and extra-curricular activities requires a sensitivity not only to the rhythms of the academic semester but also to the rhythms of the various yearly religious observances. On any given day, students' minds, hearts, and bodies are involved in academic settings but they are also participating in the daily and seasonal practices of their faith tradition. Is it Ramadan when Muslim students are fasting? Is it Advent when Christians are in eager anticipation of the celebration and feasting of Christmas? Is it the holy Days of Awe between Rosh Hashanah and Yom Kippur when Jews celebrate the birth of the world, the New Year of Years, yet simultaneously enter a 10 day period of self-assessment and repentance?

What does it mean to be in a community that honors the various religious observances and practices of the "other"? How do we respect difference and diversity while at the same time seek common ground? Designed for a North American audience, this book does not presume to cover all that is present in the North American context, let alone around the globe. We clearly recognize that not all practicing Jews, Christians, or Muslims will

---

[1] The University of the West (a Buddhist institution) is also part of our collaborative and Claremont School of Theology had a Center for South Asian Religions. While the hope is that one day a book like this will be expanded to include the yearly ritual observances of Buddhists, Hindus, Sikhs, Jains, Baha'is, etc., here we focus solely on the three Abrahamic traditions.

5

follow/participate in all the "occasions" we include in this book, and we are sure there are practices within various denominations/subgroups that have been omitted. Some will feel that we have included too much that is observed by only a small minority, and some may feel that we haven't covered enough. Yet we still believe that bringing the ritual cycles of practitioners of the Abrahamic religions into conversation with one another is an important undertaking alongside the study of the history, beliefs and sacred texts of each of these religions that can readily be found elsewhere. As we seek to understand our neighbors who are rooted in one of these three traditions, it is important to know something of their metanarrative that undergirds their observances, their emotional rhythms at different times of the religious year, the foundational sacred texts, symbols and symbolic acts.

This book is primarily a handbook for religious leaders and laity interested in being sensitive to those friends, neighbors, and co-workers who practice one of these three religions. What follows are brief descriptions documenting the important feasts/holidays/seasons or holy occasions that guide the yearly observances of each faith tradition. The three chapters begin with an overview of the calendar, important background information, and a short synopsis of the metanarrative that is the underlying framework for the yearly ritual cycle. What follows is a list of common topics for each occasion, though not all topics relate to every religion or occasion within a religion's yearly observances. The topics included are:

Name of the "occasion" (feast/holiday/season/holy day/day of remembrance, etc.)

Begins/Ends: *When does the "occasion" begin and end?*
Purpose: *What is the purpose of the "occasion"? What does it honor, celebrate, remember, inaugurate?*

Theological Emphasis: *What religious or theological themes are highlighted during this "occasion"?*

Important Texts: *What are the sacred or historical texts that provide the story behind this "occasion" or that are commonly read during this "occasion"?*

Preaching/Teaching: *Does this "occasion" usually include preaching or some other form of speech/lecture/proclamation/teaching?*

Moods: *What are the emotional moods or tones that are associated with this "occasion"? Is this a time of celebration and rejoicing or a time for repentance or a time of mourning?*

Primary Symbols (not included for Islam): *In Judaism and in Christianity, are there symbols that are usually associated with this particular "occasion"?*

Primary Symbolic Gestures or Symbolic Acts: *Are there symbolic gestures or symbolic actions that are often performed/done during this "occasion"?*

Required, Recommended or Optional: *Is participation in/adherence to this particular "occasion" considered a requirement by one's tradition or is it recommended or something that only a particular subset of people would participate in?*

Restrictions: *Are there any restrictions associated with this "occasion"? While usually this would refer to whether one could/should go to one's job during the "occasion," there may be other restrictions to consider.*

Common Customs: *Are there common customs associated with the "occasion" that take place outside the worship/prayer context?*

Fasting/Feasting Practices: *Are practitioners of the religious tradition encouraged to fast or feast in connection to this "occasion"?*

Foods: *Are there particular foods that are commonly eaten or avoided because of this "occasion"?*

7

Additional Worship/Prayer/Ritual Services or Special Focus for Regular Weekly Worship/Prayer: *Are there any additional worship/prayer times /rituals that take place for this "occasion"? Is there a specific theme or focus during the regular weekly gathering for prayer/worship that would be highlighted that would tie to the "occasion"? Are there unique prayers or songs that are included in worship/prayer time because of this "occasion"?*

The final chapter "Comparisons and Conclusions" addresses the discoveries made in the creation of this book – the "aha!" moments that occur when learning about another tradition's practices that sparks recognition of one's own in its similarity or difference.

The Jewish Year

Diversity within Judaism:

There are three main denominations within Judaism in the United States and a few smaller ones. There is also a sizable number of Jews who identify as Jewish by culture and ancestry, though not religiously, and do not affiliate with any of these denominations.

Orthodox comprise less than .3% of the US population; 10% of the US Jewish population.

Conservative comprise .5% of the US population; 18% of the US Jewish population.

Reform comprise .7% of the US population; 35% of the US Jewish population.

Reconstructionist and Jewish Renewal Movement comprise less than .2% of the US population; 6% of the US Jewish population.

No Denominational Affiliation comprise 30% of the US Jewish population.

Though statistically very small, there are also minor branches to Judaism: Renewal, Humanistic, and Transdenominational.

Note: 22% of the US Jewish population identify as Jews with no religious affiliation (secular Jews).[1]

Because these particular denominational terms (Orthodox, Conservative, Reform, etc.) are not used globally, it is difficult to estimate what the worldwide population is of persons who affiliate with one of these denominations. Outside North America, "distinctions are

---

[1] Pew Research: Religion and Public Life Project; data from Dec. 2012. http://www.pewforum.org/2012/12/18/global-religious-landscape-jew/ Accessed 3-16-15.

often made between Haredi or Ultra-Orthodox Jews, Modern Orthodox Jews and less traditional forms of Judaism."[1] In addition, when discussing Jewish Prayer, distinctions are usually made between the Sephardi and Ashkenazi liturgical traditions. "Traditional" is sometimes used to refer to both Conservative and Orthodox Jews, especially when it comes to liturgical matters. Those two denominations' siddurim (liturgical compilations) differ very little compared to Reform and Reconstructionist versions.

Celebrated by all Jews, Rosh Hashanah, Yom Kippur and Pesach are considered the three most important holy days within the Jewish Calendar. Even nominal Jews often attend prayer services and other activities on Yom Kippur and Pesach. In an effort to be comprehensive, you have outlined the maximalist (Orthodox) approach, acknowledging that practitioners will be more or less selective and varied in their approaches.

Hebrew Pronunciation Guide:

In order to help you imagine how the Hebrew words sound, below is a short pronunciation guide:

ch as in the German "ach"
g as in "goat"
a or ah as in "papa"
e or eh as in "get"
i as in "clean"
o as in "stove"
u as in "rule"
ei as in "veil"

---

[1] Pew Research: Religion and Public Life Project; data from Dec. 2012. http://www.pewforum.org/2012/12/18/global-religious-landscape-jew/ Accessed 10-12-14.

Important Vocabulary:

G-d: G-d is often used to refer to "God" in the Jewish tradition. It is true that in the Hebrew alphabet, there are no vowels but it is more than just the linguistic characteristics of Hebrew that causes many Jews to use "G-d" instead of "God". Judaism does not prohibit speaking or writing a name of God but it does prohibit defacing a name of God. When the word "God" is written down, there is also the possibility that one reading it will mistreat the word/ink/paper and thereby deface the name of God. Therefore, throughout this document, God will be spelled G-d.

Festival and Holiday Terms:

Full Festival Days: Full festival days are those festivals when no "work" is permitted: Rosh Hashanah, Yom Kippur, and the three Pilgrimage Festivals.

Pilgrimage Festivals: The three occasions known as "Pilgrimage Festivals" are Pesach (Passover), Shavuot (Pentecost), and Sukkot.

Minor Holidays: Purim and Chanukah are the most regularly observed of minor holidays, being significant observances but work is permitted. Purim is one day, Chanukah is 8 days in length.

Major and Minor Fast Days. There are five fast days, the most important being Yom Kippur and Tisha B'Av, a full 25-hour fast. Another commonly observed fast is the Fast of Esther, preceding Purim.

Days of Awe/High Holidays/High Holy Days: These three terms are used relatively interchangeably to refer to the span of time between Rosh Hashanah and Yom Kippur. This period coincides with the 10 days of Penitence known as 'Aseret Yemei Teshuvah.

Shabbat: The holy day for Jews that begins at sunset on Friday evenings and continues until sunset on Saturdays.

Terms Associated with the Jewish Bible:

Ark: The Ark is the central focus in synagogue architecture as it is the place where the Torah Scrolls are housed.

Torah: Torah is the name given to the collection of the first 5 books of the Jewish Bible: Genesis, Exodus, Leviticus, Numbers, and Deuteronomy. This collection can also be referred to as the Pentateuch. Torah can also refer to the full collection of Jewish teaching.

Nevi'im: The Nevi'im include the Jewish Bible books known as the Prophets: the Former Prophets – Joshua, Judges, Samuel, and Kings; the Latter Prophets – Isaiah, Jeremiah, and Ezekiel; and the 12 Minor Prophets – Hosea, Joel, Amos, Obadiah, Jonah, Micah, Nahum, Habakkuk, Zephaniah, Haggai, Zechariah, and Malachi.

Ketuvim: The Ketuvim include the Jewish Bible books known as the Writings: Psalms, Proverbs, Job, Song of Songs, Ruth, Lamentations, Ecclesiastes, Esther, Daniel, Ezra-Nehemiah, and Chronicles.
Note that the order of the books in the Jewish Bible is different from the order of the books in the Christian Old Testament or the Christian version of the "Jewish Bible".

Terms for Synagogue Services:

Ma'ariv: Evening prayer service that takes place after sundown every night in traditional synagogues but certainly on Friday evening, the beginning of Shabbat, and other holidays.

Shacharit: Morning prayer services that take place every morning in traditional synagogues but certainly on

Saturday mornings, the main Shabbat service, and other holidays.

Minchah: Afternoon prayer services that take place every afternoon in traditional synagogues but often on Saturday afternoons of Shabbat, and other holidays.

Musaf: Often called the "Musaf service," the Musaf is an additional component to the morning service on Shabbats, the Pilgrim Festivals, Rosh Hashanah, Yom Kippur and Rosh Chodesh (every new moon which begins a new month).

Torah: The Torah includes the first five books of the Jewish Bible – Genesis, Exodus, Leviticus, Numbers, Deuteronomy. The Torah is divided into 54 "portions" so that it can be read in its entirety in one year. Because some Jewish years include a "leap month" and some don't, if there are years that don't have 54 Shabbats, "double portions" are read on two or more Shabbats so that the Torah is read through in any Jewish year.

Terms for Synagogue Prayer:

Rabbi: A rabbi is an ordained leader within the Jewish tradition. After years of education and scrutiny at various levels within the Jewish community, individuals are confirmed in their desire to become a Rabbi and are ordained as religious leaders within Judaism. In some branches but not all, ordination is accompanied by an advanced academic degree. While women are not allowed to be ordained in Orthodox Judaism, the other branches of Judaism ordain women.

Cantor or Chazzan: A cantor or chazzan is a Jewish sacred singer who is ordained or invested to lead public prayers in the synagogue. Because Jewish prayer services are primarily sung or chanted, the cantor plays an important role in Jewish ritual life. As with rabbis, cantorial training is often accompanied by an advanced academic degree. While women are not allowed to serve as cantors in Orthodox Judaism, women can be cantors in other branches.

Nusach Ha-Tefillah: Modal chant formulas used to interpret the liturgy for the various daily, festival, and holiday services. These melodic patterns change to mark the time of day, sections within a service, and the type of day on which the service is held.

Cantillation: From the Latin *cantare*, "to sing," cantillation is the public chanting from assigned biblical books. Cantillation melodies interpret signs (te'amim) found underneath and on top of the text of the Hebrew Bible. Chanted patterns vary from community to community and depending on which book is being chanted.

Haftarah: Haftarot are readings that follow the Torah reading; they are selected from the Nevi'im.

Maftir Reading: Before the Haftarah reading from the Nevi'im, there will be a final Torah reading known as the Maftir. This is done so that the Haftarah reading is never disassociated from the Torah. "Maftir" also refers to the person who has been given the honor of reading the Maftir and Haftarah readings.

Aliyah: Each time the Torah is read, the weekly or holiday "portion" is further divided into "aliyot". An Aliyah is a section of one of the readings that a member of the congregation would be invited to "read". On Shabbat, there will be 7 aliyot. Other festival days, fast days and holidays will have fewer. People are honored with an invitation to "read" an Aliyah though today, the cantor or designated reader (ba'al koreh) usually chants the Hebrew texts and those invited to "read" will offer the blessing before and after.

Amidah: Also known as the Shemoneh Esrei, the Amidah is the core prayer that is at the heart of Jewish worship. During the weekdays, it is comprised of 19 prayers: 3 introductory blessings praising G-d, 13 blessings and petitions in the middle, with three concluding blessing giving thanks to G-d. During Shabbat services, the middle section of the Amidah is reduced to one inclusive prayer because offering petitions on Shabbat places undue attention on one's own needs. Rosh Hashanah has more middle blessings than on Shabbat.

D'var Torah: A talk given by the rabbi or another service leader on topics and themes derived from the Torah portion and/or connected to themes of the day.

Shema: The Shema is a declaration of faith, an affirmation of Judaism, and Judaism's central creed.[1]

Hallel: The Hallel is a collection of six Psalms of Praise (Psalms 113-118) used on designated holidays.

Aleinu: The Aleinu is customarily sung as the closing prayer for every daily service. It talks of Israel's uniqueness among the nations in the present and looks toward a future messianic age. The Reconstructionist version omits the theme of Jewish "chosenness."

Weekly Worship:

Weekly Shabbat worship in the Jewish tradition is rooted in the weekday worship/prayer services with variations in honor of Shabbat, or any of the other festivals, fast days, or holidays.

---

[1] Donin, Hayim Halevy. *To Pray as a Jew*, location 1657-1660, p. 144.

15

The Ma'ariv (Friday evening) service:
> The Shema and its Blessings
> The Amidah
> Aleinu

The Shacharit (Saturday morning) service:
> Morning Blessings
> Verses of Song
> Shema and its Blessings
> The Amidah
> Hallel (on festivals)
> Torah Reading
> Musaf (with an additional Amidah)
> Concluding Psalms, hymns
> Aleinu

The Minchah (Saturday afternoon) service:
> Ashrei (Psalm 145)
> The Amidah
> Aleinu

Summary of the Jewish Year:
> To understand the Jewish ritual calendar, one also needs background information on how Jews identify hours, days, months, and "new years".

Jewish Hours:
> In Judaism, the "time" or start of the prayer services is often referred to as the 3rd hour or the 9th hour or the 6 ½ hour. In these instances, an "hour" is not usually 60 minutes. It is considered a "variable hour." A "variable hour" is determined by the length of daylight hours divided by 12. For example, if sunrise is at 6 am and sunset is at 8 pm, there are 14 hours of daylight or 840 minutes which, when divided by 12, would equal 70 minutes. The "variable hour" would then be one hour and 10 minutes.

But if sunset is at 8 am and sets at 6 pm, there are only 10 hours of daylight or 600 minutes which, when divided by 12 would be 50 minutes (the "variable hour"). Only when sunlight hours equals 12 will a "variable hour" equal 60 minutes. Each "variable hour" is assigned an ordinal number (1st, 2nd, 3rd, etc.). So the "3rd hour" would begin after two "variable hours" had passed.

Jewish Days:

Days in the Jewish calendar begin at sunset the night before and continue until about an hour after sunset on the day noted because the creation story in the first chapter of the Book of Genesis says "And there was evening, and there was morning, one day". Therefore, if the first day of Passover is the 15th of the month of Nisan, it actually begins at sunset on the 14th of Nisan and ends after sunset on the day noted, the 15th of Nisan. Dates are often identified by listing the month first and then the day: i.e.: Nisan 14.

Jewish Months:

The Jewish calendar is based on the lunar calendar but because the lunar calendar is roughly 354 days a year instead of 365, the various festivals and holy days would eventually rotate throughout the year. In order to keep the important festivals at certain times of the year (i.e.: to keep Pesach/Passover in the spring), the lunar calendar is modified every 7 years in a 19-year cycle. A "leap month" is added at the end of the Jewish monthly cycle in February/March to correct this shift. Therefore, every 2 or 3 years, a leap month is added known as Adar I.

Jewish New Years:

There are four "new years" in the Jewish festival calendar.
New Year for Months: The first month of the Jewish calendar is the 1st of Nisan in which occurs

17

the various preparations, prayers, and observances surrounding Pesach.

New Year for Animal Tithes: The 1st of Elul is considered the New Year for animal tithes but this new year is seldom observed any more.

New Year for Years: Rosh Hashanah, the 1st of Tishrei is the New Year for years – the beginning of Creation. It will be 5778 on Rosh Hashanah in 2017-2018.

New Year for Trees: Tu B'Shevat, the 15th of Shevat is the New Year for Trees. Because Leviticus 19:23-25 forbids eating the fruit of any tree that is less than 3 years old, planting trees and counting the age of the trees from that day forward offers a way to determine when it is legal to eat of the fruit.

The historical story or metanarrative that runs throughout the Jewish Calendar finds its textual sources in the Jewish Bible, primarily the 5 books of the Torah (Genesis, Exodus, Leviticus, Numbers, and Deuteronomy). Additional guidance on ritual practice and interpretation of the various laws comes from the Talmud which consists of the Mishnah and the Gemara. The Mishnah is the oral traditions of the Torah that were eventually codified and written down around 200 C.E. The Gemara is the compilation of rabbinical discussions on the Mishnah and Torah. The Talmud exists in two versions: Palestinian (known as the Yerushalmi), completed around 400 C.E., and the more extensive Babylonian (known as rabbis Bavli), compiled about a hundred years later. The Babylonian version has become the most authoritative for the Jewish community. The Gemara is the compilation of rabbinical discussions on the Mishnah and Torah.

The Jewish Year has different beginnings because of the New Year for months and the New Year for Years. Jewish calendars begin the year with the New Year for Years, Rosh Hashanah, which is in the fall. However, the biblical books refer to the months as "first," "second," etc. beginning in the spring.

What follows begins with the New Year for months, the first month of Nisan (usually in March or April), and the celebration of the festival of **Pesach** (Passover). After a time of preparation, Pesach celebrates the freedom of the Hebrew people from slavery in Egypt with G-d's promise of a land of their own flowing with milk and honey. It is the second most important day in the Jewish calendar. G-d hears the cries of the oppressed and calls Moses to lead the people out of Egypt. The Pharaoh resists and G-d sends ten plagues, the final one of which is the death of the first born sons of the Egyptians. For the Hebrew people who followed G-d's instructions, the angel of death "passed over" their homes and spared their sons. When the Hebrew people fled Egypt, G-d parted the sea so they could walk across on dry land. Pesach celebrates this crucial event in the life of the Jews by retelling the various parts of the narrative over a ritual meal called the Seder.

While the Exodus truly begins a life of freedom from slavery, it is not until Moses receives the 10 commandments representing the Torah that the true covenant between G-d and the Hebrew people is established. Recommitment to this covenant takes place every year at **Shavuot** (Pentecost). To keep the events of Pesach tied to Shavuot (and in remembrance of earlier agricultural offerings), the time between Pesach and Shavuot is marked by a practice called **Counting the Omer**.

For those denominations that observe it, there then follows **Three Weeks of Mourning** for the destruction of the First and Second Temples in Jerusalem but also mourning what are considered to be the two most heinous sins committed by the Jews in their relationship to G-d. The first is called the "Golden Calf" incident. When Moses did not return in a timely manner from his encounter with G-d on the mountaintop, the people became impatient and created a golden idol in the form of a calf to worship. The second had to do with disbelief that G-d could do what G-d promised: give them a land of their own. Spies scouted out the land G-d promised that was already inhabited and they didn't believe the Hebrew people would be victorious. They doubted G-d's promise. The mourning themes are reiterated on **Tisha B'Av**. **Tu B'Av** marks the end to this time of mourning. The people reconnect with G-d after their estrangement and reclaim joy.

The New Year for Years takes place in September or October. After a period of preparation, **Rosh Hashanah** begins this ten day period known as the High Holidays or the High Holy Days or the Days of Awe. Rosh Hashanah is a joyous celebration of the New Year but it is tempered by the reality that this day also inaugurates the ten day period of repentance which culminates in **Yom Kippur**, the most important day in the Jewish calendar. It is a time of self-inventory, choosing life in relationship with G-d. Yom Kippur is the Day of Atonement when one's name is written in the Book of Life and each is given a new start.

Immediately following Yom Kippur, people will begin building a sukkah for the festival that will take place five days later. A sukkah is a temporary shelter in which meals are eaten during the 7 day festival called **Sukkot**. Sukkot retells the story of when G-d provided for the Hebrew people when they had no home, little food or water, and were wandering in the desert before they reached the Promised Land. G-d's presence was with them throughout this long journey. Throughout Jewish history as people were persecuted and displaced, Sukkot reminds the community of G-d's abiding presence. The day after Sukkot is **Shemini Atzeret** which falls on the 8th day after the beginning of Sukkot, a symbolic number of completion and redemption. Shemini Atzeret is a day of great joy that celebrates the atonement attained on Yom Kippur. The following day is **Simchat Torah**, a day to celebrate the conclusion of the reading of the entire Torah and the opportunity to start a new beginning with Genesis 1:1.

Chanukah is a minor holiday that falls in the month of December or late November and celebrates light in the midst of darkness, hope when the odds are not in one's favor, and unexpected miracles of plenty. The 8 day holiday commemorates the rededication of the Second Temple in Jerusalem at the time of the Maccabean Revolt against the Seleucid Empire of the 2nd century B.C.E., and the miracle of a dedicatory flame that was lit with a day's worth of oil but lasted for eight days.

Purim closes out the Jewish calendar with the retelling of the story of Queen Esther, Mordecai, and the evil man Haman who sought the genocide of all the Hebrew people. It is a time to celebrate the victory of Esther and Mordecai and a legitimate time to mock the powerful, even those within the religious community.

There are other days of note that congregations may observe:

> Yom Ha-Shoah - Remembering the victims of the Holocaust
>
> Yom Ha-Atzma'ut - Celebrating the establishment of the State of Israel in 1948
>
> Lag B'Omer - Remembering the end of the plague that killed Jewish scholars during the lifetime of Rabbi Akiva.
>
> Sheloshet Yimei Hagbalah - Recalling the three days of restriction that were placed by G-d on the

Hebrews preceding Shavuot, when the Torah was given to Moses

Tu B'Shevat - The new year for trees that plants hope for future generations to come

Fast of Esther – A day of fasting in recognition of the role Esther played in saving the Israelites from extermination. It is commemorated from dawn until dusk on the eve of Purim.

PESACH FESTIVAL
Z'man Cheiruteinu – Season of our Freedom

Nisan (March/April) Nisan is the first month of the Jewish Festival Calendar.

Preparation for Pesach (Passover):

Begins: Between Nisan 1 and 13.

Purpose: The two weeks prior to the Pesach (Passover) festival are a time of preparation: getting one's home and food ready for the Seder meal and special dietary rules observed for the festival. According to Deuteronomy 16:3, the Israelites fled Egypt in haste and had no time to wait for the dough to rise. Therefore matzah, unleavened bread, is an essential component of Pesach and homes are cleansed of any leaven. Pesach also focuses one's inner attitude, intent, and spiritual disciplines on G-d's saving acts in the Exodus.

Primary Symbolic Acts:

Giving Charity: Since the additional costs of foods required for a Pesach Seder meal may be beyond what some people can afford, it is customary for those who can afford it to contribute to funds that will provide financial support for those who cannot.

Cleaning House: In preparation for Pesach, one's home is thoroughly cleaned and any items containing leaven (chametz) will be removed from the house.

Kashering Kitchen Items: Because there may be some residue of leaven remaining on kitchen utensils, some families will have separate utensils, vessels, and dishes that are only used for Passover. However, if not, these items are "kashered" as a way to purify them for use in the Seder meal. The form that the kashering takes (rinsing, boiling, soaking for a few days) will vary depending on the make-up of the item (metal, glass, etc.). Items made from any porous material (pottery, earthenware, etc.) is not an option for kashering since total purification is not possible.

Fast of the Firstborn: *The Fast of the Firstborn is a minor fast.*

Begins/Ends: Nisan 14 (sunset on Nisan 13 to sunset on Nisan 14).

Purpose: Commemorates the firstborn sons of the Hebrew slaves in Egypt who were spared during the tenth plague just before the Exodus.

Fasting/Feasting Practices: While this is a fast day (fasting from sunrise to sunset), only firstborn males are expected to observe it.

Erev Pesach - Pesach Eve:

Begins: Nisan 14 (sunset of Nisan 13).

Ends: Before sunset on Nisan 14 (the beginning of Pesach).

Purpose: The purpose of Pesach Eve is to perform ritual acts regarding leaven (chametz) in order to physically purify one's home for the Seder Meal that begins the Pesach festival and to spiritually purify one's life. The home must be purged of anything that could be considered chametz (leavened elements). Grain alcohols have yeast in them so they are chametz (beer, scotch, bourbon, rye). Any of the 5 kinds of grains that have come in contact with water are also considered chametz (wheat, barley, oats, spelt, rye). The ritual acts are known as: Bedikat chametz, Bi'ur chametz, and Bittul chametz. *See below under* Primary Symbolic Acts *for more detail on each of these rituals.*

Primary Symbols: Chametz/leaven.

Primary Symbolic Acts: Purifying one's home of anything considered chametz.

Bedikat Chametz: Those gathered will search the house once more to make sure there is no chametz left in the home. By the eve of Pesach, however, the house has been completely cleaned of any chametz so this search is more symbolic. If there are children in the household, a few pieces of leavened bread are usually hidden so there is actually something to find during this search of the home. The ritual of Bedikat Chametz begins soon after sundown on Nisan 13, the eve of Pesach. After a candle is lit and a blessing is recited, the house is searched. After the search has been completed, a formula for "nullification of the leaven" (Bittul Chametz) is pronounced *(see below)*. Any chametz that is found is put aside to be burned the next morning on Nisan 14 (Bi'ur Chametz) *(see below)*.

Bittul Chametz: Just in case there is still chametz in the home that no one knows about, a formula is recited which nullifies any leavened elements that were not found in the search and may still be in the house.

Bi'ur Chametz: Before the 5th hour on Nisan 14, any leavened elements that were found during the search the night before are burned outside and the ashes are considered to be "dust of the earth." The nullification formula is recited again after the leavened elements have been burned. As a symbolic tie between the festival of Sukkot and Pesach, some will use the palm branch (lulav) from Sukkot to light the fire that will destroy the leaven. *(For an understanding of the lulav, see the "Ritual of the Four Species" section under* **Sukkot** *below.)*

Mechirat Chametz: This custom applies to some who own businesses that include leavened products or who feel they have too much to make it physically or financially feasible to get rid of it all but who also want to obey the law that they must not "own" anything considered chametz during the 8 days of Pesach, the chametz items can be "sold" to a non-Jew and then bought back after Pesach. While it is not a physical exchange of property, it satisfies the religious law to not own leaven during Pesach.

Foods: Matzah (unleavened bread) is intentionally *not* eaten on the day before Pesach so that it is more special on the night of the Seder meal.

Additional Worship/Prayer/Ritual Services or Special Focus for Regular Weekly Worship/Prayer:

Shabbat Ha-Gadol: The Sabbath before Pesach is known as the "Great Sabbath" as it anticipates the upcoming Pesach festival.

Pesach (Passover): *Pesach is the second most important festival of the Jewish Year.*

The first of all festivals to occur in the Jewish Year, Pesach is also known as Chag Ha-Aviv (The Holiday of Spring) *and Chag Ha-Matzot (The Holiday of Unleavened Bread). The first two days and the last two days are full festival days. The days in between are called Chol Ha-Moed or intermediate days. *Note: for those people who were ritually impure or otherwise unable to ritually celebrate Pesach and partake of the Seder meal (Pesach Sheini), a second chance is given a month later to do so.*

Begins: Nisan 15 (sunset on the 14th of Nisan – the full moon of the Spring Equinox).

Ends: 8 days later after sunset on Nisan 22.

Purpose: Pesach celebrates the Exodus from Egypt which ended the enslavement of the Hebrew people. It also rejoices in the settling of the land promised them by G-d and the covenant between G-d and the Israelites. Pesach however, is more than a remembrance or commemoration of past events. It is a reliving, a re-enactment of those events today where each individual experiences freedom from those things that enslave and the freedom to covenant/re-covenant with G-d.

Theological Emphasis: Hope, liberation, redemption. Pesach provides the opportunity to hold fast to the hope of new possibilities in the direst of circumstances, even slavery; to give thanks for G-d intentionally acting to liberate G-d's people from slavery and oppression, and to celebrate the multiple forms of redemption past, present, and those to come (Creation, Exodus, return of exiles, Messianic Age). The story of Pesach retells the physical liberation from slavery in Egypt through the Exodus and how the covenant between G-d and the Israelites was sealed in the acceptance of the Torah revealed to Moses, but it also looks to a future time of redemption when the Messiah will come.

Important Texts: Exodus, chapters 1-15, especially Exodus 12:14-51 (narrative)

Torah Readings: Exodus. 12:21-51; Maftir Reading: Numbers 28:16-25. Haftarah Reading: Joshua 3:5-7; 5:2-6:1, 6:27.

Moods: Gratitude, liberation, renewal.

Primary Symbols:

Seder Meal: Seder means "order" and refers to the ritual ordering of the meal and the liturgy at the meal which is called the Haggadah. During the Seder, there are symbolic foods that are not eaten, symbolic foods that are eaten, ritual blessings, ritual actions and the retelling of the story of the Exodus known as the Haggadah.

The Seder Table: In addition to the plates and silverware, there will also be candles, a seder plate, a small bowl of salt water, a plate that holds three plain flour and matzah (unleavened bread) on top of each other often with a paper or cloth divider between the three, and multiple cups of wine (or "Kosher for Passover" grape juice for those unable to drink wine).

The Seder Plate: The Seder plate includes symbolic foods, some of which are eaten and some that are not:

Karpas: Karpas consists of a green vegetable (usually parsley) that symbolizes spring and new birth. During the ritual, the green vegetable is dipped in salt water representing the tears of the slaves. The Karpas is placed on the Seder plate in the lower left.

Charoset: Charoset is a dish that is a mixture of chopped nuts, apples, spices and wine (though recipes vary) and represents the mortar used by the slaves in Egypt to make bricks. It is placed on the Seder plate in the lower right.

Maror: Maror are some form of bitter herbs (often romaine lettuce or freshly ground horseradish) that symbolize the bitterness of the lives of the Hebrews during slavery. The Maror is placed in the center of the Seder plate.

Beitzah: A Beitzah is a scorched hard boiled egg that has been roasted on a stove burner until one side of it is blackened. This roasted egg represents the various festival sacrifices that were brought by the ancient Hebrews to the Temple in Jerusalem. The Beitzah is placed on the Seder plate in the top left.

Zeroa: Zeroa is a roasted bone (often a shank bone, though a broiled beet can be used for vegetarians) that symbolizes the first "paschal" lamb that was offered on the night of the Exodus. It is known as the Pesach or Passover sacrifice and is placed on the Seder plate in the top right.

Chazeret: Some plates may also include Chazeret which is usually romaine lettuce. It provides additional maror which can be used later in the "Hillel's sandwich". If used, the Chazeret is placed on the Seder plate at the bottom in the center.

Plate of 3 Matzot: Three matzot are placed on top of one another. Often a cloth or paper towel is placed between each as a type of divider.

4 Cups of Wine: There are multiple explanations as to why there are four cups of wine that are used in the Seder meal. One explanation is that they represent the four expressions of redemption found in Exodus 6:6-7: 1) the people are redeemed from the burdens of the

Egyptians, 2) they are redeemed from bondage, 3) they are redeemed with an outstretched arm, and 4) they are redeemed, taken by G-d to be G-d's people.

Elijah's Cup: Because Exodus 6:8 includes a fifth expression of redemption ("I will bring you into the land that I swore to give Abraham, Isaac, and Jacob"), there was controversy over whether there should be 5 cups of wine instead of 4 on the Seder table. The Talmud leaves this as one of the many questions for Elijah to decide in messianic times so this cup is called "Elijah's Cup". No one drinks from this cup.

Primary Symbolic Acts:

Reclining: Reclining was an historic practice of those who were free people, not slaves. To signify their freedom from slavery in Egypt, the people gathered around the table recline to the left when eating the matzah, partaking of the 4 cups, eating the "koreikh" (a sandwich made from the bottom matzah and some of the maror and chazeret), and eating the final piece of the afikomen (the half piece of the middle matzah that was found after it had been hidden).

Wearing of the Kittel: Many will wear a kittle (white robe worn in death) as a symbol of dying to one's old way of being (a slave) and being born anew (a free, liberated person).

Participating in the Seder Meal and Ritual:

Kadesh: A blessing for sanctifying the day is recited over the first cup of wine which is then drunk while "reclining". Another blessing gives thanks for sustaining us in life.

Urchatz: A ritual washing of hands.

Karpas: The vegetable (often parsley) is dipped in the bowl of salt water.

Yachatz: Using the plate of matzot which has three matzot on it, one on top of the other, the middle matzah is removed and broken in two, symbolic of the parting of the sea during the Exodus. The larger piece is wrapped in a cloth or napkin and is set aside to later become the afikoman which will then be hidden for the children to find and ransom back to the adults at the end of the meal. The smaller half is returned to the plate with the other two matzot.

Maggid: This is a ritual retelling of the story of the Exodus known as the Haggadah. There are hundreds of editions of this story available from a wide variety of perspectives and all are valued since it is considered praiseworthy to expand upon this story.

Rachtzah: A ritual washing of the hands and the recital of a blessing.

Motzi Matzah: Two blessings are recited over the three matzot on the plate: a regular one for bread and a special one for matzot. The people will then eat from the top matzah and the smaller half of the middle matzah while "reclining".

Maror: The maror is dipped in the charoset (mixture of chopped apples, nuts, spices and wine) and eaten. A blessing is said for the maror.

Koreikh: Because a wise sage named Hillel believed that the matzah and morar (bitter herbs) were eaten together in Temple times, the morar is placed on the matzah that was on the bottom of the plate to make a "Hillel's sandwich."

Shulhan Oreikh: The festive meal is eaten! Though any foods are acceptable for the meal itself, as long as they are kosher for Pesach, many begin by eating hard boiled eggs in salt water. To avoid any connection with actually eating the Pesach sacrifice, some will choose to not serve roasted meat or roasted foods of any kind.

Tzafun: When the meal is completed, the children seek out the afikomen, the larger half of the middle matzah that was wrapped and hidden. When they find it, they ransom it back to the adults and the last thing everyone eats is a small portion of this matzah as a taste of the future redemption to come. While more cups of wine will be drunk, no more eating will take place after eating the afikomen.

Bareikh: Grace is said after the meal and then there is a blessing over the third cup of wine which is drunk while "reclining".

Elijah's Cup: A child will open the door to the house in hopes that Elijah will come in. Elijah is the one who will announce the coming of the Messiah and the final redemption. An ornate cup, known as Elijah's Cup, will be placed on the table. There is another blessing before and after the 4th cup of wine which is then drunk while "reclining".

Hallel: During hallel, 6 Psalms of praise are recited (Psalms 113-118).

Nirtzah: The ritual ends with part of a poem "Chasal Siddur Pesach", singing or saying

"Next year in Jerusalem," and singing songs common to Pesach.

Restrictions: Eating or owning chametz (leavened items) is forbidden. Depending on one's level of observance, no work is allowed on the first two and last two days of the festival.

Common Customs:

Greetings: It is customary to greet one another with Gut Yontif (Good Holy Day), Chag Sameach (Happy Festival), or Happy Passover!

Fasting/Feasting Practices: Feasting.

Foods: Eating of Matzah is prescribed.

Additional Worship/Prayer/Ritual Services or Special Focus for Regular Weekly Worship/Prayer:

Evening Service. At the end of Nisan 13 there will be the regular Minchah (afternoon) service with the beginning of the Pesach festival on Nisan 14 taking place at the Ma'ariv (evening) service. The Minchah service will usually take place just before sunset and the Ma'ariv just after sunset so the people can attend both services.

Morning Service. Held on Nisan 15, this Shacharit service (if held on a weekday) will include a portion from Exodus 34:6-7 which talks about the 13 divine attributes of G-d which are recited three times. Hallel is also recited. There is an additional unique Prayer for the Dew which connects Pesach to the new birth of springtime that is part of the history of the development of the festival of Pesach and another Prayer is added that prays for the Redeemer to come to establish the Kingdom of G-d.

Day 2 of Pesach: *Day 2 of Pesach is a full festival day for Orthodox and those Conservative and Reconstructionist*

Jews who choose to observe it. For Reform Jews, Day 2 is not considered a full festival day with all the requirements and restrictions involved. Pesach, then, becomes a 7 day festival rather than an 8 day festival.

Begins/Ends: Nisan 16 (sunset to sunset on the 15th/16th).

Important Texts: Pesach, Day 2: Torah Reading: Leviticus 22:26-23:44. Maftir Reading: Numbers 28:16-25. Haftarah Reading: II Kings 23:1-9, 21-25.

Symbolic Acts:

> Seder Meal: For those who observe this day as a full festival day, the Seder Meal will be repeated. It may also be repeated by those who don't observe the day as a full festival but choose to gather with friends and family for the meal and to re-tell the Exodus story.

Additional Worship/Prayer/Ritual Services or Special Focus for Regular Weekly Worship/Prayer:

> Counting the Omer: The services are the same as for Pesach, Day 1, except at the end of the Ma'ariv service on the 2nd Day of Pesach, the "Counting of the Omer" will begin. *(For detailed description of "Counting the Omer," see below.)*
>
> *For those who observe Day 2 of Pesach as a full festival day, the services are the same as on Pesach, Day 1 and the Seder Meal will be repeated.*

Chol Ha-Moed - Intermediate Days of Pesach:

The four days in-between are known as chol ha-moed or intermediate days of the festival.

Begins: The second day of Pesach.

Ends: The 7th Day of Pesach.

Important Texts:

> Chol Ha-Moed, Day 1/3rd Day of Pesach: Torah Reading: Exodus 13:1-16; Maftir Reading: Numbers 28:19-25.

Chol Ha-Moed, Day 2/4th Day of Pesach: Torah Reading: Exodus 22:24-23:19; Maftir Reading: Numbers 28:19-25.

Chol Ha-Moed, Day 3/5th Day of Pesach: Torah Reading: Exodus 34:1-26; Maftir Reading: Numbers 28:19-25.

Chol Ha-Moed, Day 4/6th Day of Pesach: Torah Reading: Exodus 9:1-14; Maftir Reading: Numbers 28:19-25.

Shabbat Chol Ha-Moed: Torah Reading: Exodus 33:12-34:26; Haftarah Reading: Ezek. 37:1-14. Some will recite the book of the Song of Songs before the Torah reading.

Additional Worship/Prayer/Ritual Services or Special Focus for Regular Weekly Worship/Prayer:

"Half" Hallel: While the services are basically the same as the first two days of Pesach (except for the readings), the 6 Psalms of Praise (Hallel) will be shortened in order to recognize that freedom from slavery of the Israelites during the Exodus also meant the deaths of the many Egyptians who drowned after the parting of the sea. The joy of this day is tempered or limited because of these deaths and therefore the Psalms of Praise are likewise limited.

Restrictions:

Eating Chametz: People will refrain from eating chametz (leavened foods).

Weddings: Some congregations restrict weddings during these days so the joy of the wedding festivities won't overshadow the extended Pesach festival.

Mourning the Dead/Eulogies: Because of the joy of this season, some will withhold the giving of eulogies during this time and will postpone sitting shiva (mourning rituals after death) until after Pesach.

Fasting/Feasting Practices: Continued eating of matzah.

Pesach, Day 7: *Day 7 of Pesach is a full festival day.*

Begins: Nisan 21 (sunset on the 20th).

Ends: After sunset on the 21st of Nisan.

Purpose: As a full festival day, Pesach Day 7, continues the celebrations of this season.

Theological Emphasis: Same emphasis as the rest of the holiday.

Important Texts: Torah Reading: Exodus 13:17-15:26. Maftir Reading: Numbers 28:19-25. Haftarah Reading: II Samuel 22:1-51.

Symbolic Acts:

Additional Worship/Prayer/Ritual Services or Special Focus for Regular Weekly Worship/Prayer:

"Half" Hallel

Yizkor or Memorial Services for the Deceased

In Israel and according to Reform custom,

Yizkor is recited on the seventh day. In other denominations, it is recited on the eighth day. There will be a time where those who have died will be remembered and honored. In some congregations, those whose parents are still alive will leave during this part of the service.

Last Day of Pesach, Day 8: *Day 8 of Pesach is a full festival day.*

Begins: Nisan 22 (sunset on the 21st).

Ends: After sunset on the 22nd of Nisan.

Purpose: Continues the celebrations of Pesach.

Theological Emphasis: Same emphasis as Pesach.

Important Texts: Torah Reading: Deuteronomy 15:19-16:17; Haftarah Reading: Isa. 10:32-12:6. If the 8th day falls on Shabbat, the Torah Reading is: Deuteronomy 14:22-16:17 with the Haftarah Reading remaining the same.

Restrictions: No work

Additional Worship/Prayer/Ritual Services or Special Focus for Regular Weekly Worship/Prayer: "Half" Hallel

Counting the Omer: *An "omer" is a unit of measure for grain brought to the temple as an offering on the 16th of Nisan.*

Begins: The second night of Pesach, Nisan 17 (sunset on the 16th).

Ends: After sunset on the last day of Iyar/1st of Sivan.

Purpose: Counts the days between Pesach and Shavuot. While Pesach celebrates freedom from slavery and the Exodus out of Egypt, Shavuot is when the true covenant with G-d is established when the Torah is given to Moses. To keep the two events tied together as one story, the days between the two festivals are counted.

Theological Emphasis: Claiming liberation from slavery, it is a time to prepare to freely choose the covenant of the Torah for oneself.

Important Texts: Leviticus 23:15; Psalm 67.

Moods: Because of a plague during the lifetime of Rabbi Akiba (a renowned rabbi in the Talmud), some Jews observe this period as a time of partial mourning where people refrain from weddings, parties, dancing, etc.

Primary Symbols: Numeric counting of seven days in a week times seven weeks.

Primary Symbolic Acts:

Recitation of the Counting: At the close of the Ma'ariv service, there is the nightly recitation of the formula for counting the "omer": i.e.: "Today is 9 days, which is one week and two days of the Omer;" or "Today is 31 days, which is three weeks and three days of the Omer."

Recitation of Psalm 67: Some will recite Psalm 67 because it symbolically represents 49: there are seven verses with a total of 49 words in it.

Restrictions: Some observe this as a period of mourning, and thus refrain from weddings, parties, dancing, etc.

Additional Worship/Prayer/Ritual Services or Special Focus for Regular Weekly Worship/Prayer:

Sefirot: There are sefirot, "characteristics" or "emanations" of G-d's being, that are experienced in the world and biblical ancestors who have embodied these. Each characteristic is also tied to virtues and vices which are found in each of us. During the Counting of the Omer, Jews examine their lives to identify the vices, and mourn them so they can let go of them and strive for the virtues so they can more fully experience the sefirot of G-d.

Divine Sefirot	Archetypal Person	Virtue	Vice
Hesed (Grace)	Abraham	Love	Lust
Gevurah (Severity)	Isaac	Respect	Fear
Tiferet (Beauty)	Israel	Compassion	Indulgence
Netzah (Victory)	Moses	Efficiency	Pedantry

Hod (Glory)	Aaron	Aesthetics	Vanity
Yesod (Foundation)	Joseph	Loyalty	Promiscuity
Malkhut (Majesty)	David	Surrender	Stubbornness[1]

Yom Ha-Shoah:

Begins/Ends: Nisan 27 (sunset to sunset Nisan 26/27).

Purpose: To remember the 6 million Jews who died in the Holocaust.

Theological Emphasis: This is a day of intentionally questioning G-d, even judging G-d, for the horrors of the Holocaust. It is a day when one's theology and relationship to G-d is challenged and re-examined.

Moods: Mournful, reflective.

Iyar (April/May)
Yom Ha-Atzma'ut:

Begins/Ends: Iyar 5 (sunset to sunset Iyar 4th/5th) – the date of the founding of the state of Israel in 1948.

Purpose: To celebrate the return of the land to the Jewish people, from which they were expelled by the Romans in 135 C.E.

Lag B'Omer:

Begins/Ends: Iyar 18 (sunset to sunset Iyar 17th/18th); the 33rd day of counting the Omer.

Purpose: A minor festival to commemorate the symbolic end of the plague that killed Jewish scholars during the lifetime of Rabbi Akiva.

---

[1] Strassfeld, Michael. *The Jewish Holidays: A Guide & Commentary*. NY: HarperCollins Publishers Inc, 1985; HarperResource Quill paperback edition, 2001; Kindle location 1508.

Moods: Any mourning practices that have been observed during the Omer period are suspended on this day.

Common Customs: Outdoor outings and picnics are common on Lag B'Omer.

Sivan (May-June)
Sheloshet Yimei Hagbalah – Three Days of Restriction:
Begins: Sivan 3 (sunset on the 2nd).

Ends: Sunset on Sivan 5.

Purpose: The Three Days of Restriction recalls the three days the people prepared themselves on Mt. Sinai and the limitations of movements and actions G-d placed on the people before Moses went up the mountain to receive the 10 Commandments, commemorated on Shavuot.

Important Texts: Exodus 19:10-25 (narrative).

Moods: Devotional.

Restrictions: none

Common Customs:

Ritual Bath: Because one of the commands of G-d during this time of preparation and restriction was to wash, some will purify themselves at the "mikveh," the ritual bath, on the day before Shavuot.

Additional Worship/Prayer/Ritual Services or Special Focus for Regular Weekly Worship/Prayer:

Shabbat Kallah: the Shabbat before Shavuot. *"Shabbat Kallah" is also the name given to any Shabbat before a wedding. It highlights the covenant relationship/marriage between G-d and the Israelites at Sinai.*

Shavuot (Pentecost): *Shavuot means "Weeks".*

Shavuot is also known as Chag Ha-Bikkurim (the Festival of the First Fruits) and Chag Matan Torateinu (the Festival of the Giving of Torah).

Begins: Sivan 6 (sunset on the 5th).

Ends: Sunset on Sivan 7.

Purpose: Shavuot marks the culmination of the Exodus. The journey of the Israelites celebrated during Pesach began as slaves in Egypt, then liberation from bondage and oppression in the exultant crossing of the sea. But it is not until Moses receives the law on Mt. Sinai that the true covenant between G-d and the Hebrew people is sealed. Shavuot marks this moment of divine/human contact and the revelation of the Torah to Moses.

Theological Emphasis: Revelation; covenant. G-d revealing the Torah to Moses and the Israelites accepting it seals the covenant began by G-d in the Exodus.

Important Texts: Leviticus 21:15-16, 21(narrative); often the Book of Ruth

Shavuot, Day 1: Torah Reading: Exodus 19:1-20:23; Maftir Reading: Numbers 28:26-31; Haftarah Reading: Ezekiel. 1:1-28, 3:12.

Shavuot, Day 2: Torah Reading: Deuteronomy 15:19-16:17; Maftir Reading: Numbers 28:26-31; Haftarah Reading: Habakkuk 3:1-19.

Moods: Reverential, rededication.

Primary Symbols:

Torah: The Torah is especially revered on this day in celebration of the covenant it enacts between G-d and the Israelites.

Greenery: Green plants, branches, even trees are often used to decorate the synagogue and peoples' homes.

Roses and Spices: Rose is the flower associated with Shavuot. Rose petals and spices may be scattered throughout the synagogue to add a pleasing aroma.

Papercuts: Papercuts in flower and tree designs are a form of folkart that often decorates the synagogue and homes during Shavuot.

Primary Symbolic Acts:

Procession with Torah Scroll: The service leader carries the Torah scroll around the synagogue in a procession.

Leavened Bread: To signal a good harvest as well as to mark the move from the unleavened matzah of Pesach (which represented poverty) to the bread of affluence, leavened bread may be waved before the altar.

Restrictions: No work permitted.

Common Customs:

Study of the Torah: In the Kabbalistic tradition, there is a custom of studying the Torah all night long or they rise early for a sunrise service.

Confirmation/Graduation Ceremonies: For youth aged 16 or 17, confirmation marks the affirmation of commitment to the Jewish people. For other communities, Jewish high school graduation ceremonies may take place on Shavuot.

Foods:

Eating dairy products and honey: Rooted in a wide variety of traditions and rationales, eating cheeses, blintzes, other dairy products as well as honey is common on Shavuot.

Additional Worship/Prayer/Ritual Services or Special
Focus for Regular Weekly Worship/Prayer:

Hallel: The 6 Psalms of Praise (Psalms 113-118)
known as "hallel" are included in the synagogue
service on Shavuot.

Book of Ruth: The Book of Ruth is read on the
second day of Shavuot.

Ten Commandments: The 10 Commandments are
included in the Torah service of the first day
of the festival. People usually stand in honor
of this gift from G-d that Shavuot celebrates.

Yizkor: The memorial service for the dead is recited
following the Torah and Haftarah readings.
In Israel, Yizkor is recited on the first (and
only) day of Shavuot.

Tammuz and Av (June-July)
Fast Days - 3 Week Mourning Period:

Begins: Tammuz 17 (sunset on the 16th).

Ends: after sunset on Av 9.

Purpose: To mourn the destruction of the First Temple
(586 B.C.E.) and Second Temple (70 C.E.). It is also a
time to mourn two of the worst sins depicted in the
Torah: 1) "The golden calf" incident (Exodus 32:1-10)
which took place while the people were waiting for
Moses to return from Mt. Sinai. When Moses didn't
return in a timely manner, the people became
impatient and made a golden calf as an idol that they
would worship, and 2) "Disbelief of the Spies"
incident in which the spies who were sent to scout
out the land of Canaan promised by G-d to the
Israelites did not believe they would be victorious in
defeating the Canaanites. As a result, the older
generation died in the desert and only the children

entered the Promised Land "flowing with milk and honey" (Exodus 3:8).

Theological Emphasis: Lament.

Important Texts: *There are Shacharit (morning) and Minchah (afternoon) services for the Fast Days.*

Shacharit: Torah Reading: Deuteronomy 4:25-40; Haftarah Reading: Jeremiah 8:13-9:23.

Minchah: Torah Reading: Exodus 32: 11, 34:1-10; Haftarah Reading: Isa. 55:6-56:8.

Moods: Solemn remembrance; mourning; grief.

Restrictions: While there are no work restrictions during this time, weddings and other celebrations are not usually held during these Three Weeks of mourning.

Common Customs:

Shoah/Holocaust Remembrance: Some synagogues will also mourn those who died in the Shoah during this period.

Fasting/Feasting Practices: Tammuz 17 and Av 9 (the first and last days) are both minor fast days (fasting from sunrise to sunset). Also, except for Shabbat meals, many will refrain from eating meat or drinking wine from Av 1 through Av 9 (known as the Nine Days).

Foods: Foods that are commonly eaten by those in mourning over the death of a loved one will also be eaten during this period: hard-boiled eggs and lentils.

Av (July-Aug)
Tisha B'Av:

Begins/Ends: Av 9 (sunset to sunset on the 8th/9th).

Purpose: Tisha B'Av ends the three week period of mourning. It reiterates the destruction of both temples and remembers major tragedies that have befallen the Jewish people.

Important Texts: Book of Lamentations.
> Sharharit (morning service): Torah Reading: Deuteronomy 4:25-40; Haftarah Reading: Jeremiah 8:13-9:23.

Minchah (afternoon service): The texts are the same as other fast days (Torah Reading: Exodus 32:11-14, 34:1-10; Haftarah Reading: Isaiah 55:6-56:8 (only at Minchah service).

Moods: Solemn remembrance; mourning; grief.

Restrictions: While there are no work restrictions on Tisha B'Av, in addition to fasting (no food or water), people may not bathe, wear any scents (perfumes, aftershave lotion, oils), engage in sexual relations, or wear leather (shoes, coats, etc.). People will also refrain from greeting one another on this day of mourning. It is the one day in the year when people are encouraged *not* to study the Torah. Only reflection on the Book of Lamentations (Eichah) which describes the destruction of Jerusalem in 586 B.C.E., portions from the Talmud and the book of the prophet Jeremiah that deal with the destruction of Jerusalem are allowed.

Common Customs:
> Draping the Ark (Torah Cabinet): A black cloth is often draped over the Ark.

> No Wearing Tallit and Tefillin: Ordinarily during morning services (shacharit), it is customary for people to wear the tallit (fringed shawl wrapped around one's shoulders) and the tefillin (leather pouches containing stylized hand-written verses from the Torah tied around one's arm and one's head). These are not worn during Tisha B'Av because the glory they represent is absent on this day.

Fasting/Feasting Practices: Like Yom Kippur, Tisha B'Av is a full fast day which means people fast for 25 hours beginning before sunset the night before and continuing until after sunset.

Additional Worship/Prayer/Ritual Services or Special Focus for Regular Weekly Worship/Prayer:

> Book of Lamentations: The entire Book of Lamentations will be read during the Ma'ariv Service. People may sit on the floor or on low benches for this reading.

> Kaddish: Kaddish is a prayer in the Aramaic language that is most notably associated with mourning. The Kaddish Yatom, prayer for mourners, is recited as the Three Weeks of Mourning comes to a close.

Tu B'Av:

Begins/Ends: Av 16 (sunset to sunset on the 15th/16th).

Purpose: It serves as the end of this symbolic "shivah" period (the 7 days of mourning for the dead) for those who mourned for the Three Weeks. It marks the beginning of putting aside the various customs associated with mourning and reclaiming joy and celebration. In Israel, it is celebrated as a day of love, similar to Valentine's Day.

Theological Emphasis: Reconnecting with G-d after being estranged from one another during the weeks of mourning.

Moods: Mourning turning to joy.

Elul (Aug-Sept)

Preparation period for Rosh Hashanah and Yom Kippur:

Begins/Ends: Encompasses the entire month of Elul.

Purpose: Self-examination of one's relationship with G-d and with others.

Theological Emphasis: Penitence and forgiveness.
Important Texts: Psalm 27.
Moods: Spiritual introspection.
Primary Symbols:

> The Shofar: The shofar is usually made out of a ram's horn (connecting the shofar to the ram that G-d provided to Abraham to be sacrificed instead of Isaac). It should be curved or bent to represent a bent or humble spirit. It is blown as a type of horn to call people to repentance.

> The Color White: A white Parokhet (ark covering) and reading table cover are exchanged for the regular covers because white symbolizes purity and atonement as people anticipate the upcoming Days of Awe.

Primary Symbolic Acts:

> Blowing the Shofar: After every morning Shacharit service, the shofar is blown except on Sabbaths and the day before Rosh Hashanah.

Common Customs:

> Hatarat Nedarim: "Hatarat Nedarim" is a practice whereby two or three persons covenant together to be honest with one another as each undertakes the process of self-inventory, identifying one's strengths and weaknesses, and turning one's life more toward G-d.

> Visit Graves of Parents: Originally, people visited the graves of their parents in hopes that they would intercede on their behalf as the time of judgment approached when G-d determined whether one's name would be listed in the Book of Life or not. Today, some still visit the graves of their ancestors.

> Greeting: People begin to wish each other "shanah tovah" – a good New Year.

Additional Worship/Prayer/Ritual Services or Special
Focus for Regular Weekly Worship/Prayer:

Psalm 27: Psalm 27 is recited at the end of morning
and evening services.

Selichot: the week before Rosh Hashanah, special
penitential prayers seeking forgiveness (selichot)
are recited. The primary prayer is repeated
several times and is based on Exodus 34:6-7
which lists various merciful attributes of G-d.

DAYS OF AWE

Tishri (Sept-Oct)
Rosh Hashanah, Day 1:

Begins: Tishri 1 (sunset on Elul 29). It falls on the 7th new
moon after Nisan (the first month of the Jewish Year).
Since 7 is an important number in Judaism, it is a
special new moon.

Ends: After sunset on the 2nd of Tishri *(Most Reform Jews
only celebrate Rosh Hashanah for one day, Tishri I).*

Purpose: Celebrates the beginning of creation, the
birthday of the world which tradition places on
Tishri 1. It is the New Year for Years (Nisan is the
New Year for Months). It is the Day of Sounding the
Shofar (Yom Teruah) and the Day of Remembering
(Yom Ha-Zikaron). Rosh Hashanah marks the
beginning of a 10 day period of repentance.

Theological Emphasis: Repentance (teshuvah); the
Sovereignty of G-d.

Important Texts: Leviticus 23:23-25 (narrative).
Torah Reading: Genesis 21:1-34; Maftir Reading:
Numbers 29:1-6; Haftarah Reading: I Samuel 1:1-
2:10.

Moods: There is a mixture of moods on Rosh Hashanah.
On the one hand it is a serious, somber day of self-

inventory, reflection, and repentance. On the other hand, it celebrates the birth of the world and the readings highlight births of important ancestors. It also gives thanks for second chances to repent and have one's name sealed in the Book of Life. So joy and solemnity are held in tension on this day.

Primary Symbols:

> The Shofar: Made from a ram's horn, representing the ram that G-d provided as a sacrifice in lieu of Abraham's son, Isaac, the shofar is used as a horn during Rosh Hashanah.

> Book of Life: The Book of Life is a symbol of those whose faithfulness to G-d in this life promises communion with G-d in the afterlife. Rosh Hashanah is a time for people to recommit themselves to G-d and to have their name written in the Book of Life where it will be verified and sealed on Yom Kippur.

> The Color White: The "parokhet" (ark covering) and cover of the reading table continue to be white during this period.

Primary Symbolic Acts:

> Blowing the Shofar: Each day of Rosh Hashanah one hears the blasts of the Shofar (100 blasts is customary). There are rhythms and patterns to the blowing of a shofar, collectively called "teki'ot". A "tekiah" constitutes one long blast. "Shevarim" means that the shofar will be blown in three short blasts. Nine staccato blasts is called "teru'ah". The traditional pattern for blowing the shofar includes a combination of these rhythmic sounds in three distinct sets. It is important to note that in traditional synagogues if the first day of Rosh Hashanah falls on Shabbat, the shofar is not sounded at all.

48

Prostration: The act of prostration takes place once during the service on Rosh Hashanah. Prostration requires kneeling and touching one's forehead to the ground.

Restrictions: No work permitted.

Common Customs:

Tashlikh: During the afternoon of Rosh Hashanah, some will seek out a body of water that has a current (river or ocean rather than pond or small lake), and throw bread crumbs into the water as a symbol of casting away one's sins.

Foods:

Apples and Honey: Some will dip apples in honey and eat.

Avoiding Nuts: Because the letters that form the word for nuts in Hebrew, "egoz," is the numerical equivalent of the word for sin, many refrain from eating nuts on Rosh Hashanah.

Other Foods to Avoid: Some will avoid acidic and sour foods.

Additional Worship/Prayer/Ritual Services or Special Focus for Regular Weekly Worship/Prayer:

Texts: The story of the birth of Isaac (Genesis 21:1-7) is read on the first day of Rosh Hashanah. The Talmud connects the birth of Isaac, the birth of Samuel, and the births of Jacob and Esau to Rosh Hashanah. Birth images connect to the birth of the world celebrated on this day.

Two Torah Scrolls: As on all full festival days, two Torah scrolls will be removed from the ark and read from and there will be five aliyot (assigned readings/verses read by different people) instead of three. *(Five is the norm for holy days/festivals.)*

Musaf Service: In addition to the Ma'ariv (Shabbat evening), Shacharit (morning), and Minchah (afternoon) services, there will be an additional Musaf Service that will take place as there is for any holiday in traditional practice.

Amidah of Musaf: The central portion (Amidah) of the additional service (Musaf) held on Rosh Hashanah is unique in that it has three central berakhot (blessings) which speak theologically of G-d. The first is called "malkhuyot" which highlights the sovereignty of G-d or G-d as King of the Universe who created the world and reigns over it and all humankind. The second is called "zikhronot" and portrays G-d as the one who remembers the faithful acts of the ancestors and remembers all the good and bad things that were said and done. The third, "shofarot", connects texts involving the shofar and recalls the past revelation of G-d found in the Torah revealed to Moses on Mt. Sinai and looks to the future promised revelation when the Messiah comes and the final redemption at the end of days.

Omission of Hallel: Despite the fact that Rosh Hashanah is a festival day and festival days include "Hallel" (the 6 Psalms of Praise from Psalms 113-118), Hallel is omitted on Rosh Hashanah because the solemnity of the day does not allow for the joy expressed in Hallel.

"Choose Life" Theme: Since the days between Rosh Hashanah and Yom Kippur are days for people to repent of their sins and choose a faithful way of living, people are encouraged to "choose life". When one chooses life over death (living away from the law of G-d), one's name is written/sealed in the Book of Life on Yom Kippur.

Rosh Hashanah, Day 2: *Note: Some liberal congregations in America may only observe 1 day.*

Begins/Ends: Tishri 2.

Purpose: Commemorates Abraham's willingness to sacrifice his son, Isaac.

Important Texts: Rosh Hashanah, Day 2: Genesis 22:1-24 (narrative).

    Torah Reading: Genesis 22:1-24; Maftir Reading: Numbers 29:1-6; Haftarah Reading: Jeremiah 31:1-19.

Restrictions: No work permitted.

Additional Worship/Prayer/Ritual Services or Special Focus for Regular Weekly Worship/Prayer:

    Shacharit and Minchah Services: Both are the same as the first day of Rosh Hashanah except for the readings.

'Aseret Yemei Teshuvah - 10 Days of Penitence:

Begins: Tishri 2.

Ends: After sunset on Tishri 9.

Purpose: For those who are not totally righteous or totally evil (whose fates are already sealed in the Book of Life or the Book of Death), the 10 Days of Penitence between Rosh Hashanah and Yom Kippur provide people further opportunity to repent and seek G-d's forgiveness before Yom Kippur when names are symbolically sealed in the Book of Life.

Theological Emphasis: Repentance.

Moods: Solemnity, self-evaluation and increased devotion.

Common Customs:

    All Night Prayer: Some will go to the synagogue at night and stay until dawn reciting prayers and making supplications.

    Seeking Forgiveness from Others: Because Yom Kippur is a time when sins between humans and

G-d are forgiven but not sins between humans and each other, many will seek to repair damages to relationships during the 10 days of Penitence so that on the day of Yom Kippur, one may truly start anew.

Additional Worship/Prayer/Ritual Services or Special Focus for Regular Weekly Worship/Prayer:

Selihot: Penitential prayers are recited every morning.

Tzom Gedalliah – the Fast of Gedalliah:

Begins/Ends: Sunset to sunset on Tishri 2nd/3rd.

Purpose: Commemorates the assassination of the Jewish governor of Judah and the destruction of the first temple in 586 B.C.E.

Fasting/Feasting Practices: A minor fast from sunrise to sunset to mourn the destruction of the first temple.

Shabbat Shuvah – the Sabbath of Turning or the Sabbath of Repentance:

Begins/Ends: The Shabbat that falls between Rosh Hashanah and Yom Kippur.

D'var Torah: Instead of a sermon offered during the morning Shacharit service, the sermon is often given during the afternoon Minchah service.

Erev Yom Kippur:

Begins: Tishri 9 (sunset on the 8th).

Ends: Until sunset on Tishri 10 – the beginning of Yom Kippur.

Purpose: The time to make final preparations before Yom Kippur.

Theological Emphasis: Confession and Repentance.

Common Customs:

Confession: Prayers of confession (viddui) are recited.

Seudah ha-mafseket: Eating the last meal before the 24 hour fast.

The Memorial Light: A memorial light will be lit in honor of deceased parents and continue to burn throughout Yom Kippur.

Wearing White: Women often wear white.

Blessing of Children: Before going to Kol Nidrei (beginning evening service of Yom Kippur), parents often bless their children wishing them a good year formed by a moral and ethical life.

Yom Kippur – Day of Atonement: *Yom Kippur is the most important/most sacred holiday.*

Begins/Ends: Tishri 10 (sunset to sunset on the 9th/10th).

Purpose: There are multiple purposes to Yom Kippur: to respect G-d's judgment, celebrate the assurance of forgiveness, and to give thanks for being able to wipe the slate clean and start over in one's covenant with G-d.

Theological Emphasis: Judgment and atonement - sins are forgiven (between the individual and G-d, not between the individual and other people) and Jews begin anew.

Important Texts: Leviticus 16:30 (narrative). *See below for texts important to specific services on Yom Kippur.*

Moods: Most solemn day of the Jewish year.

Primary Symbols:

Book of Life. On Yom Kippur, G-d's judgment is symbolically entered in the Book of Life with names inscribed in it.

The Color White: Often the officiants will wear white on Yom Kippur. It is also possible that others will wear white clothing as a symbol of purity.

Restrictions: No work, no eating or drinking, no bathing, no anointing of the body with oil, no wearing leather shoes, no sexual relations, no cooking.

Common Customs:

> Greetings: "Have an easy fast" and/or "Gemar hatimah Tovah" - "A good final sealing [to you]".

> Wearing the Kittle: Because Yom Kippur is a time when people face their own mortality, some will wear the white "kittle" - a robe that is worn in death.

> Begin Construction of Sukkah: In order to tie the festival of Yom Kippur to Sukkot (the next festival 5 days later), some will begin building the Sukkah after the conclusion of Yom Kippur.

Fasting/Feasting Practices: All those of a religiously mature age (12 for girls; 13 for boys) and who are not compromised by poor health are expected to fast for 25 hours beginning before sunset on the afternoon/evening before Yom Kippur and ending after nightfall on the day of Yom Kippur.

Additional Worship/Prayer/Ritual Services or Special Focus for Regular Weekly Worship/Prayer: *While there are five services on Yom Kippur, they are considered one long, continuous service. The final service, Neilah, is unique to Yom Kippur and concludes this most holy day of the Jewish Year.*

> *Kol Nidrei:*

> > Begins: Because the Kol Nidrei service includes the annulment of vows between humanity and G-d (which cannot take place on a Sabbath or festival day), this service begins before sunset on Tishri 9.

> > Purpose: A time to focus on the cleansing of one's will.

Primary Symbolic Acts:

Chanting: The Kol Nidrei text is dramatically chanted three times with increasing volume each time it is chanted to a melody unique to this service.

Common Customs:

Tallit and Kittel: For those who wear the tallit (fringed shawl wrapped around one's shoulders) and/or kittel (white ceremonial robe) on Yom Kippur, they are put on before the Kol Nidrei service and worn for all 5 services. The Kol Nidrei service is the only evening service in the Jewish Year where a tallit is worn.

Additional Worship/Prayer/Ritual Services or Special Focus for Regular Weekly Worship/Prayer:

Opening Prayer: The service is given the name Kol Nidrei because these are the words of its opening prayer which is written in Aramaic, not Hebrew.

Annulment of Vows: There is a time in the service when promises made between the self and G-d that have not been kept are proclaimed null and void. This acknowledges that human beings often fall short of the life they intend to lead. This only refers to vows made in regards to Judaism (its ritual, customs, law) or to oneself (regarding personal conduct, refocusing one's life for the good, etc.). The annulment of vows does not involve promises and vows made to other people.[1]

Ma'ariv:

Begins: After sunset on Tishri 9.

Purpose: While this is a regular evening service, the emphasis is on remembering and reliving the atonement rites historically done in the Temple.

Common Customs:

Beating of One's Breast: On this most holy of days when repentance and atonement take center stage, some may choose to beat their breast.

Shacharit:

Begins: The morning of Tishri 10.

Purpose: A time to focus on the cleansing of one's mind.

Important Texts: Torah Reading: Leviticus 16:1-34; Maftir Reading: Numbers 29:7-11; Haftarah Reading: Isaiah 57:14-58:14.

Additional Worship/Prayer/Ritual Services or Special Focus for Regular Weekly Worship/Prayer:

Yizkor Prayers: Memorial prayers for the dead will be recited during the Shacharit service.

Reminding G-d: There are devastating acts throughout the history of the Jewish people that should never have occurred. During this service on Yom Kippur, the people

---

[1] Strassfeld, Michael. *The Jewish Holidays: A Guide & Commentary*. NY: HarperCollins Publishers Inc, 1985; HarperResource Quill paperback edition, 2001; Kindle location 5261.

remind G-d that G-d has not always "remembered his own mercies".[1]

Six Aliyot: Six people will be invited to read rather than the usual 5 for the other Festival days.

Musaf:

Begins: afternoon of Tishri 10. This is the longest service of the Jewish Year.

Purpose: A time to focus on the cleansing of one's heart.

Additional Worship/Prayer/Ritual Services or Special Focus for Regular Weekly Worship/Prayer:

Avodah Service: The Avodah service gives a detailed description of the prayers and ceremonies on Yom Kippur in the Temple service before its destruction. Highlighted from this service is a recitation of the confession of the High Priest where the High Priest repented of his own sins, those of the other priests, and those of the entire Israelite community. In this confession, the High Priest would pronounce the ineffable name of G-d and the people would prostrate themselves before G-d's name. Today, some synagogues continue this practice by having the reader fall prostrate during the recitation of the High Priest's confession.

---

[1] Strassfeld, Michael. *The Jewish Holidays: A Guide & Commentary.* NY: HarperCollins Publishers Inc, 1985; HarperResource Quill paperback edition, 2001; Kindle location 3417.

Martyrology: After the destruction of the Temple, the martyrdom of Jews became more pronounced. During this service, a poem about the martyrdom of 10 Sages is recited and some will include commentary on the millions martyred in the more recent Nazi Holocaust.

Omission of Normal Concluding Elements: Because the five services on Yom Kippur are really one long, continuous service, normal concluding elements such as the aleinu (the closing prayer for all services) or hymns are not included in the Musaf service.

Minchah:

Begins: afternoon on Tishri 10 after the Musaf service.

Important Texts: Torah Reading: Leviticus 18:1-30; Haftarah Reading: Jonah 1:1-4:11, Micah 7:18-20.

Additional Worship/Prayer/Ritual Services or Special Focus for Regular Weekly Worship/Prayer:

Torah Reading: The Minchah service on Yom Kippur begins with the Torah reading. Only one scroll is removed from the ark from which three people will be invited to read passages.

Haftarah Reading: The third reader of the Torah texts will also read the Haftarah (readings of the Prophets). The Haftarah is the entire book of Jonah because it emphasizes the power of repentance and reaffirms that no one can escape the presence of G-d. The last three verses of the book of Micah are also read as part of the Haftarah reading.

Neilah: *Neilah means "closing" (referring to the closing of the gates).*

Begins: Afternoon on Tishri 10 after the Minchah service.

Purpose: This service is unique to Yom Kippur and is the shortest service of the Jewish Year. It takes the congregation symbolically to the gates of heaven with one last chance to do teshuvah (repentance). It is the closing service of Yom Kippur.

Primary Symbolic Acts:

Keeping the Ark Open: Some synagogues will keep the ark open throughout the Neilah service but since people stand whenever the ark is open, congregations with older members may choose to keep it open for a shorter period of time.

Final Blowing of the Shofar: The final blowing of the shofar for Yom Kippur heralds the end of the fast but it also recalls the ancient tradition of announcing the Jubilee Year on Yom Kippur with the blowing of the shofar. While the blowing of the shofar is traditionally done at the end of the Neilah service, some synagogues postpone this significant act until the end of the Ma'ariv service that follows. Once the shofar is blown to signify the end of Yom Kippur, many will not stay for the Ma'ariv service. Postponing the blowing of the shofar until the end of Ma'ariv encourages people to stay.

Additional Worship/Prayer/Ritual Services or Special Focus for Regular Weekly Worship/Prayer:

Additional Prayers: There are two additional prayers that are included in the Neilah service that highlight G-d's mercy in welcoming sinners who repent.

Moods: While the beginning of Neilah maintains the solemn tone of the entirety of the Days of Awe, at the end of Neilah, the people leave in a joyous mood. They have been forgiven of their sins, their names have been written in the Book of Life, and the fast has ended!

Ma'ariv: The regular weekday Ma'ariv evening service will take place after the Neilah service though because it is immediately following Yom Kippur, it takes on additional significance.

Preparation for Sukkot:

In the five days between Yom Kippur and Sukkot, each family will build a sukkah (a temporary shelter called a booth or tabernacle), gather the "four species," consisting of three types of branches and an "etrog" (a lemon-like citrus fruit) in preparation for Sukkot rituals. Often the synagogue will also build a sukkah outside.

Building a Sukkah: A sukkah requires temporary walls (roughly between 3 feet and 30 feet high and a minimum of 26 inches square) and a removable roof. The roof, called a "sekhakh," cannot be solid and should be made of material that grows out of the earth so it is often made of branches. It is important to be able to see the sky. The custom is to decorate the sukkah so each can be very unique in its appearance. The sukkah should be first used on Sukkot eve. Most people don't sleep in the sukkah but they will eat in the sukkah.

Preparing the Four Species: The "Four Species" are actually 7 different items: one palm branch (lulav), two myrtle branches (hadassim) and 3 willow branches (avavot) at least 12 inches high with the palm branch about a third higher than the others. They are collectively called the "lulav" because the palm branch dominates. All the branches need to be fresh rather than dried. They are tied together with the palm branch in the middle, the willow branches on the left and the myrtle branches on the right. They are placed in a holder with the spine of the palm branch facing the holder. Then there is one citron fruit called an "etrog" which is similar to a lemon but has a tapered top and a rougher skin. It needs to be about the size of an egg and yellow in color.

Preparing the Hoshanah: The Hoshanah is a collection of 5 willow branches (separate from the ones in the lulav of the four species).

Night before Sukkot: Some will spend the night before Sukkot in study as part of their preparation for this festival.

Sukkot – Festival of Booths: *Sukkot means "tabernacles".*
Sukkot is the third and final pilgrimage festival in the Jewish Year (along with Pesach and Shavuot). It also is the culmination of the High Holiday cycle. The first two days are full festival days.

Begins: Tishri 15 (sunset on the 14th).

Ends: After sunset on Tishri 21.

Purpose: In addition to fulfilling a commandment to build a hut and reside in it for 7 days, Sukkot remembers the impermanence of the Israelites' wandering in the wilderness and the presence of the divine that guided them. It recognizes the impermanence of life that is likewise dependent on the presence of the divine. Sukkot also looks toward the final redemption at the end of time.

Theological Emphasis: G-d's abiding presence. Though homeless in the desert wilderness, one is always at home in G-d; though exposed to the elements, G-d provides shelter.

Important Texts: Leviticus 23:39-43 (narrative).

Sukkot, Day 1: Torah Reading: Leviticus 22:26-23:44; Maftir Reading: Numbers 29:12-16; Haftarah Reading: Zachariah 14:1-21.

Sukkot, Day 2: Torah Reading: *same reading as Day 1*; Maftir Reading: *same reading as Day 1*; Haftarah Reading: I Kings 8:2-21.

Chol Ha-Moed (intermediate day), Day 1/3rd Day of Sukkot: Torah Reading: Numbers 29:17-25 (4 readers - aliyot);

Chol Ha-Moed (intermediate day), Day 2/4th Day of Sukkot: Torah Reading: Numbers 29:20-28 (4 readers - aliyot).

Chol Ha-Moed (intermediate day), Day 3/5th Day of Sukkot: Torah Reading: Numbers 29:23-31 (4 readers - aliyot).

Chol Ha-Moed (intermediate day), Day 4/6th Day of Sukkot: Torah Reading: Numbers 29:26-34 (4 readers - aliyot).

Shabbat Chol Ha-Moed: Torah Reading: Exodus 33:12-34:26; Maftir Reading: Numbers 29; Haftarah Reading: Ezekiel 38:18-39:16. Often the Book of Ecclesiastes will be read on the Shabbat of the intermediate days of Sukkot.

Moods: Joy and thanksgiving.

Primary Symbolic Acts:

"Residing" in the Sukkah: While most people don't actually live in the sukkah, they will eat in the sukkah, say the festival version of the "Kiddush" (prayer that sanctifies the day) over the wine, bless the sukkah with the prescribed blessing, perform a ritual washing of the hands, and recite a blessing over the bread.

Ritual of the Four Species: People bring their lulav (with all 6 branches in the holder) and their etrog (the lemon-like fruit) with them to the synagogue on Sukkot. The lulav is placed in the right hand with the spine of the palm holder facing the one holding it. The etrog is in the left hand with the tapered end pointing down. Then a blessing that names the commandment to wave the palm branch sanctifying the people of Israel is recited. The etrog is then turned right side up with the tapered end facing up and the lulav is "waved" or "shaken" for a total of six times: twice during the reading of Psalm 118:1, twice during the reading of Psalm 118:25, and twice during the reading of Psalm 118:29. One "wave" or "shake" of the lulav and etrog consists of pointing them in front (to the east) and shaking three times, then pointing them to one's right (south) and shaking three times, then pointing them over one's shoulder (west) and shaking three times, then pointing them to one's left (north) and shaking three times, then lifting them above and shaking three times and finally holding them low and shaking them three times.

Common Customs:

Inviting Ushpizin: Ushpizin are symbolic guests that are invited to the sukkah every day. Each are biblical ancestors who were wanderers or exiles and a different one is invited each night: Abraham, Isaac, Jacob, Joseph, Moses, Aaron, David (Sarah, Rachel, Rebecca, Leah, Miriam,

Abigail, and Esther for those who also include women ancestors).

Using Dried Lulav for Pesach: Some will save the dried palm branch or willows from the four species to use to burn the leavened "chametz" found cleaning the house in preparation for Pesach. This ties the end of the High Holiday cycle to the beginning of the next festival at Pesach.

Fasting/Feasting Practices: Eating in the sukkah is very important during Sukkot. Some will travel from sukkah to sukkah, eating and drinking a small portion before moving on to visit another sukkah.

Foods: Wine, bread, cake.

Additional Worship/Prayer/Ritual Services or Special Focus for Regular Weekly Worship/Prayer:

Circuiting the Synagogue: Hoshanot prayers/hymns are said/chanted and the congregation repeats each line responsively. Hoshanot are those prayers/hymns that begin with "hoshanah," meaning "save us." During these prayers, the leader also holds the four species and circuits the synagogue once. Those members of the congregation who have made their own lulav and etrog follow behind the leader in the procession then return to their seats. This takes place while the Torah Scroll is on the bimah and the ark is open.

Book of Ecclesiastes: The entire book of Ecclesiastes will be read on Sukkot.

Hoshanah Rabbah - *means the Great Hosanna:*

Begins/Ends: Sunset to sunset, Tishri 20/21. It is known as the 7th Day of Sukkot.

Purpose: This is the last day of Sukkot and the absolute closing of the Book of Life, the final judgment day. For some, Hoshanah Rabbah marks the ultimate conclusion of the High Holiday period.

Important Texts: Torah Reading: Numbers 29:26-34.

Moods: While the festival of Sukkot is a time of joy and celebration, the day of Hoshanah Rabbah also carries a penitential tone.

Common Customs:

    Wearing Fine Clothes: It is common to wear good clothes on Hoshanah Rabbah. The cantor will often where a kittel to draw a connection to the Days of Awe.

Additional Worship/Prayer/Ritual Services or Special Focus for Regular Weekly Worship/Prayer:

    Torah Scrolls: Many or all of the Torah scrolls are taken from the ark on this day.

    Circling Synagogue: The Four Species will be processed around the synagogue 7 times during the recitation of the hoshanah prayers.

    Beating the Hoshanah (Willows): During the additional, penitential hymns, the four species are set aside and the hoshanah (5 willow branches) is beat against the ground to signify the fragility of life (the leaves fall off) but the sun and rain sent by G-d produce new leaves. G-d also provides new life in one's struggle to survive.

Shemini Atzeret:

Begins/Ends: Tishri 22 (sunset to sunset on the 21st/22nd).

Purpose: It is the day following the last day of Sukkot which means it is the 8th day. The 8th day has special symbolism in that it represents the actual day/moment of redemption (as opposed to the *promise* of redemption).

Important Texts: Torah Reading: Deuteronomy 14:22-16:17; Maftir Reading: Numbers 29:35-30:1; Haftarah Reading: I Kings 8:54-9:1.

Moods: Joyful celebration.

Restrictions: No work permitted.

Additional Worship/Prayer/Ritual Services or Special Focus for Regular Weekly Worship/Prayer:

Musaf Service: During the Musaf service on Shemini Atzeret, a prayer for rain is recited because the origins of this day are rooted in agricultural rituals seeking sufficient rainfall for the coming winter months.

Full Festival Day Practices are in effect for Shemini Atzeret.

Yizkor: The memorial service for the dead is recited following the Torah and Haftarah readings. In Israel, Yizkor is recited on the combined Simchat Torah/Shemini Atzeret.

Simchat Torah:

Begins/Ends: Tishri 23 (sunset to sunset on the 22nd/23rd).

Purpose: Celebrates the completion of the yearly reading of Torah.

Theological Emphasis: Torah as companion in the life of the individual and the community.

Important Texts:

Shacharit morning service: Torah Reading: Deuteronomy 33:1-34:12; Genesis 1:1-2:3; Maftir

Reading: Numbers 29:35-30:1; Haftarah Reading: Joshua 1:1-18.

Moods: Joyful celebration.

Primary Symbols: The children will pass out symbolic Torah scrolls. Flags may be present that represent the tribes of Israel who wandered in the desert.

Primary Symbolic Acts:

Torah Procession: The leader, holding the Torah, followed by others holding the Torah scrolls, processes around the synagogue. A responsive prayer is recited between the leader and the congregation. As the Torah passes members of the congregation, they may "kiss" the Torah by touching their tefillin or a scarf to the Torah and then kissing the tefillin or scarf. At the end of the procession, singing and dancing ensues! All but one of the Torah scrolls are returned to the Ark (residing place of the Torah). One is kept out to be used during the rest of the service.

Torah Reading:

Aliyah: The Torah readings are divided up and someone in the congregation is invited to "read" a portion. This reading by invitation is called an "aliyah". On Simhat Torah, everyone is invited to "read" from the Torah so Deuteronomy 33:1-26 is read repeatedly.

Children's Aliyah: This is the only day of the year when children are honored by being allowed/invited to read from the Torah.

Groom of the Torah: The last verses of Deuteronomy 33:27-34:12 is the final reading. The person given the honor of reading these verses is known as the "Groom of the Torah".

Hagbah: To symbolize "turning" the Torah back to the beginning" (Genesis 1:1), a person holds

67

the Torah in a unique way. With hands crossed, the scroll is lifted and turned so that the writing faces the congregation.

Additional Worship/Prayer/Ritual Services or Special Focus for Regular Weekly Worship/Prayer:

Shacharit Morning Service: As a holiday, it has its own Amidah (central portion of the service) and Hallel (6 Psalm of Praise) that are recited.

Reading of the Torah: This is the only night in the year when the Torah is read at night during the Ma'ariv (evening) service.

Cheshvan (Oct-Nov)

Kislev (Nov-Dec)

Chanukah: *Chanukah means "dedication" (Note: Chanukah is primarily observed in the home.).*

Begins: Kislev 25 (sunset on the 24th).

Ends: 8 days later in the month of Tevet. Since the number of days in the month of Kislev varies from year to year (29-30 days), the ending date of Chanukah also varies. Chanukah can end on Tevet 2 or 3.

Purpose: Celebrates the victory of a small band of Maccabees against a large army of Greeks in 167 B.C.E. after King Anitochus Epiphanes forbade Sabbath rituals and forced everyone to become hellenized. The Maccabees won independence from the Greeks. It also celebrates the miracle of a cruse of oil that burned 8 days when there was only enough oil for one day. Chanukah, which means "dedication", also recalls the dedication of the Temple where the miracle of the oil occurred.

Theological Emphasis: Light in the midst of darkness; hope in the midst of devastation; plenty in the midst of scarcity.

Important Texts: I and II Maccabees (narrative)
Day 1: Torah Reading: Numbers 7:1-17.
Day 2: Torah Reading: Numbers 7:18-29.
Day 3: Torah Reading: Numbers 7:24-35.
Day 4: Torah Reading: Numbers 7:30-41.
Day 5: Torah Reading: Numbers 7:36-47.
Rosh Chodesh, Day 6: Numbers 28:1-15, 7:42-47.
Day 7 (not Rosh Chodesh): Torah Reading:
      Numbers 7:48-59.
Day 7 (Rosh Chodesh): Torah Reading: Numbers
      28:1-15; 7:42-47.
Day 8: Torah Reading: Numbers 7:54-8:4.
Shabbat Chanukah: regular portion. Maftir Reading:
   Torah Reading for the day is read as the maftir;
   Haftarah Reading: Zechariah 2:14-4:7. If there is a
   second Shabbat of Chanukah, the Haftarah
   Reading is Kings I 7:40-50.
Moods: Victorious, celebratory.
Primary Symbols: Menorah, candles, light.
Primary Symbolic Acts:
   Lighting of the Menorah: The Menorah consists of
      eight candles plus a "shammash" candle which is
      used to light the other candles and is placed
      higher than the other eight. Every night (after
      dark but before midnight) a blessing is recited
      and then a new candle is lit. Candles are lit from
      the right to the left. The new light is lit first and
      then any candles from previous nights are lit
      from left to right (i.e.: the candle representing
      tonight is lit first, then the candle that represented
      last night is lit, and then the one from the night
      before, etc.). Songs are often sung after the
      lighting. The candles should stay lit for a half
      hour. The lighting of the Menorah takes place in
      peoples' homes as well as in the synagogue.

When lit in the synagogue, the Menorah is often placed on the south wall where it originally resided in the Temple in Jerusalem.

Common Customs:

Gift Giving: It is common to give gifts to loved ones during Chanukah. Often this takes place after the lighting of the Menorah.

Dreidel Game: A dreidel is a four-sided top that has a different Hebrew letter on each side: nun, gimel, heh, and shin. These letters are the first letters of the phrase: "Nes Gadol Hayah Sham" – "A great miracle happened here!" But in Yiddish the letters represent the words "nit" (nothing), "gantz" (all), "halb" (half), and "shtell" (put). While there are different ways to play the game, the basic idea is that the players begin by putting a coin (often made of chocolate, called "gelt") in a pot. If a person spins and the top lands on the nun, nothing happens. If it lands on the gimel, the person gets all of the coins. If it lands on the heh, the person gets half and if it lands on the shin, the spinner has to put another coin in the pot. When the pot is empty, everyone adds another coin. The game is won when one person has all the coins.

Foods: Foods fried in oil (to remember the miracle of the oil), especially potato latkes and sufganiyah, a type of jelly doughnut originating from North Africa.

Additional Worship/Prayer/Ritual Services or Special Focus for Regular Weekly Worship/Prayer:

Hallel: Hallel (6 Psalm of Praise: Psalm 113-118) is recited every day of Chanukah.

Zot Chanukah:

Begins/Ends: The last day of Chanukah.

Common Custom: Some dedicate the last day of Chanukah to women and read the Book of Judith.

Tevet (Dec-Jan)
Asarah B'Tevet - Fast Day:
Begins/Ends: Tevet 10 (sunset to sunset on the 9th/10th).

Purpose: Commemorates the siege of Jerusalem by Nebuchadnezzar II of Babylonia in 588 B.C.E.

Important Texts: Torah Reading: Exodus 32:11-14, 34:1-10; Haftarah Reading: Isaiah 55:6-56:8 (only at Minchah service).

Fasting/Feasting Practices: A minor fast day from sunrise to sunset.

Shevat (Jan-Feb)
Tu B'Shevat – the New Year for the Trees:
Begins/Ends: Shevat 15 (sunset to sunset on the 14th/15th).

Purpose: Honors ties to Eretz Yisrael (the land of Israel) and contemplates the future that one's children will inherit. It is also one of the 4 "New Years" in the Jewish calendar. It marks the beginning of spring.

Theological Emphasis: Rootage in ancestral lands.

Important Texts: Deuteronomy 8:8 that speaks of fruits and grains.

Moods: Reflection on the ancestral lands of the past while planning for future generations.

Primary Symbols:
Trees: Because trees often have a lifetime beyond several generations, they symbolize eternity.

Common Customs:
Plant Trees: Parents often give trees to their children to plant.

Foods:
> Fruits and grains associated with Israel: grapes, olives, pomegranates, figs, wheat, and barley.
> Nuts (especially almonds).
> Carob (also known as St. John's bread).

Adar I (leap years only) (Feb-Mar)

Adar (Adar Beit/Adar 2 in non-leap years) (Feb-Mar)
Fast of Esther:
Begins/Ends: Adar 13 (sunset to sunset on the 12th/13th).
Purpose: Commemorates the 3 days Esther fasted before she pleaded with her husband, King Ahasuerus, to stop the planned genocide of her people, the Jews.
Fasting/Feasting Practices: A minor fast day from sunrise to sunset.

Purim: *Purim means "lots". Haman casted lots to decide when the Jews would be massacred.*
Begins/Ends: Adar 14 (sunset to sunset on the 13th/14th).
Purpose: Celebrates the victory of Mordechai and Queen Esther over wicked Haman (a top official in the king's court) who planned to massacre the entire Jewish population in the kingdom.
Theological Emphasis: good over evil; power of remembering.
Important Texts: Book of Esther (narrative).
Torah Reading: Exodus 17:8-16.
Moods: "Mardi Gras" type of mood – silly, flamboyant, noisy, boisterous.
Primary Symbols: Masks, groggers (noisemakers).
Common Customs:
> Masquerades and Carnivals: Costumes, masks, and noisemakers are crafted for parades, parties, and plays or parodies.

"Roasts": While rabbinic teachers are highly respected in the Jewish community, on Purim it is acceptable to "roast" these revered members of the community.

Purim Torah: In order to maintain the Torah as a living faith and not turn it into an idol, Purim is also a time in the year when mockery of the tradition is accepted.

Fasting/Feasting Practices: Feasting takes place on the afternoon of Purim and celebrates the end of Purim. This feast is second only to the Pesach seder meal.

Foods:

Hamantaschen: Since Haman's hat was considered to be triangular in shape, Hamantaschen are triangular shaped cookies filled with a variety of things.

Kreplach: A soup filled with triangular shaped noodles filled with cheese or meat.

Additional Worship/Prayer/Ritual Services or Special Focus for Regular Weekly Worship/Prayer:

Ma'ariv: Purim begins with the evening service.

Reading from the Book of Esther: In the reading of the story from the Book of Esther, when the name of Haman is mentioned, it is common for people to make a lot of noise to drown out his name.

The Christian Year

Diversity within Christianity:

There are hundreds of different Christian groups, denominations, sects, and offshoots that have emerged since the beginning of the church. The details of this history can be found in various textbooks but for our purposes here, we will identify the three main divisions within Christianity:

> *Orthodox Christians* comprise .6% of the US population; .8% of Christians in the US; 11.9% worldwide.
>
> *Roman Catholics* comprise 23.9% of the US population; 30.4% of Christians in the US; 50.1% worldwide.
>
> *Protestants* comprise 52.3% of the US population; 65.4% of Christians in the US; 36.7% worldwide.[1]

---

[1] Pew Research – Religion and Public Life Project statistics accessed 10-10-14 at http://religions.pewforum.org/affiliations; http://www.pewforum.org/2011/12/19/global-christianity-exec/. Orthodox Christians fall primarily into two branches: Eastern Orthodox and Oriental Orthodox Churches. Within these branches there are various "limbs": Russian, Greek, Coptic, Ethiopian, Syrian, Slavic, Eritrean, etc. Protestant Christians have hundreds of denominations and many that consider themselves non-denominational. Historically in the U.S., the most prominent are called "mainline protestant denominations": the American Baptist Church, Christian Church (Disciples of Christ), The Episcopal Church, Evangelical Lutheran Church of America, the Moravian Church, the National Association of Congregational Christian Churches, the Presbyterian Church (USA), the Reformed Church in America, the United Church of Christ, and the United Methodist Church.

Celebrated by all denominations, Easter (Resurrection) and Christmas (Nativity) are considered the two most important holy days within the Christian Calendar. Though some of the Orthodox dates for Christmas and Easter (as well as the preparatory seasons of Advent and Lent) vary from those of Roman Catholicism and Protestantism (because they are rooted in the older Julian calendar rather than the Gregorian calendar which is the civic calendar used in much of the world today),[1] all three groups will make the celebration of these two events in the life of the church grand ritual occasions. Even nominal Christians often attend worship on Christmas Eve or Christmas Day and Easter Sunday.

Orthodox Christians, Roman Catholics, and many Protestants will also celebrate the "Christian Year" (also known as the Liturgical Calendar) with its various seasons and ritual observances. There are, however, many Protestant denominations and local congregations that will *only* observe Christmas and Easter, omitting the other observances throughout the year. Orthodox Christians, Roman Catholics, and a very small number of Protestant denominations (i.e.: Lutherans, Anglicans/Episcopalians) will also follow a yearly calendar celebrating "Saints Days", remembering human beings (from biblical times forward) that have been canonized/recognized by the

---

[1] The date of Easter is always determined by the Julian calendar for Orthodox Christians and the Gregorian calendar by all other Christians. The date of Christmas varies according to those branches of Orthodox Christianity that follow the older Julian calendar and those following the Gregorian calendar. Those within the Christian community that follow the older Julian calendar for the date of Christmas are the Eastern Orthodox Churches (except for the Slavic Church) and the Coptic, Ethiopian, and Eritrean Churches within the Oriental branch of Christian Orthodox Churches. Those that follow the Gregorian calendar are Protestants, Roman Catholics, and the Armenian, Syrian, and Indian Churches within the Oriental branch of Christian Orthodox churches, and the Slavic church within the Eastern Orthodox branch.

Church as a martyr and/or saint (an unusually holy person). Most often called "Feast Days," the number and names of these saints vary across denominations. Many other Protestants will celebrate all the "saints" of the church (not just those who have been canonized) on one day, All Saints Day.

Despite the differences between Orthodox Christianity, Roman Catholicism, and Protestantism as well as the myriad differences *within* each of these branches of Christianity, there is a common "Christian Year" that is observed in varying degrees by a large majority of Christians, though the specific dates, times, and practices may vary. Non-denominational and evangelical Protestants may only observe Christmas and Easter while Roman Catholic and Orthodox Christians will observe saints' days and other occasions not listed here. Practices will also vary from culture to culture. What follows is an attempt to capture the broad strokes of the occasions that tell the Christian narrative.

The important thing to note about the Christian Year is that weekly Sunday worship is first and foremost the primary ritual observance. It was on Sunday that Jesus arose from the dead and thereafter every Sunday is considered "a little Easter" where we celebrate the new life offered through the resurrection of Jesus.

Because the vast majority of Christians in the United States observe the important days and seasons of the Christian Year according to the Gregorian Calendar (rather than the older Julian Calendar), the Gregorian dates will be used in this document with notations on the differences, when deemed necessary.

Important Vocabulary:

Jesus: Considered by most Christians to be the son of God born of a virgin named Mary (the mother of Jesus) conceived by the Holy Spirit.

Holy Spirit: The spirit of God which is the third part of the Trinity.

Trinity: The Godhead is understood to be one entity with three "persons": God (often referred to as the Father), Jesus (the Son), and the Holy Spirit.

Christ: "Christ" means "messiah" but is often used as a synonym for the resurrected Jesus. While many Christians use the combined term Jesus Christ, "Christ" is not Jesus' last name. The more appropriate formulation would be "Jesus, the Christ," Jesus, the messiah.

Resurrection: Christians believe that Jesus was crucified on a cross and died but resurrected three days later. That day is celebrated as Easter.

Bible: The sacred scriptures of Christians. It contains the Old Testament/Hebrew Bible and New Testament. While all Christians agree on the 27 books found in the New Testament of the Christian Bible, there is a difference of opinion in regards to the number of books in the Hebrew Bible (often called Old Testament) portion of the Christian Bible. In the 1500s, during the Protestant Reformation, Protestants removed 10 books (Deuterocanonical) that they considered to be interesting recent history (from 400 years before Jesus was born to about 27 years before Jesus) but not inspired by God in the same way or that contained theological doctrines not supported by the Protestant Reformation. Roman Catholics eventually removed two of these 10 books but kept most of the original collection of the more recent texts, known as the

Deuterocanonical books (known by Protestants as the Apocrypha). The Orthodox Bible contains 9 of these additional Deuterocanonical books plus Psalm 151 depending on the branch within the Orthodox Church (Eastern or Oriental) and on the denomination within the branch (i.e.: Coptic, Armenian, etc.). Current Christian Bibles now range from 39 to 49 books depending on whether one is a Protestant, Roman Catholic, or Orthodox Christian.

Gospels: Books in the Christian New Testament that tell of the birth, life, ministry, death, and resurrection of Jesus.

Sacraments: A sacrament is an outward sign of an inward and spiritual grace that was instituted by Jesus and entrusted to the church. Almost all Christians (a few Protestant denominations among the exception) have two sacraments: Baptism and Eucharist/Holy Communion/Lord's Supper. Roman Catholics also include Confirmation, Reconciliation/Penance, Matrimony, Ordination, and Anointing of the Sick (previously referred to as Extreme Unction) as sacraments. While much of what the Church does can be considered sacramental according to Orthodox Christians, throughout history, Eucharist and often baptism have been considered sacraments. Though never officially voted upon by Orthodox branches of Christianity, over time, the seven sacraments of the Roman Catholic Church came to be seen as among the sacred mysteries of the church. Today Orthodox Christians often refer to either the "one" (Eucharist) or "many" (7 sacraments of the Roman Catholic Church) in referring to the sacraments.

Baptism: Baptism is an initiation rite in the Christian Church. It involves vows (statements of belief), water, and pledges by the congregation to support the new Christian. While some Protestant denominations only allow baptism for persons who are old enough to take the vows themselves, Roman Catholics, Orthodox Christians and other Protestants baptize infants. Persons being baptized will be will be immersed in water or have water sprinkled or poured on their head. In baptism, one dies to the old way of being and begins a new life with Jesus, is cleansed from sin, receives the gift of the Holy Spirit to help guide one's life, and is incorporated into the community of faith (called the "Body of Christ") that tries to live as if the future reign of God has already come on earth.

Eucharist/Holy Communion/Lord's Supper: Different denominations will refer to this liturgical action by different terms. Eucharist means to "give thanks". "Holy Communion" emphasizes the community of Christ gathered around a table for fellowship. "Lord's Supper" remembers an event in the life of Jesus (called the Last Supper) where Jesus asks his disciples to "do this in remembrance of me." "Doing *this*" means to break bread, distribute it to those gathered, and have them eat of the bread remembering the life of Jesus when he was embodied on this earth. Then to take wine and to drink from the cup remembering the blood of Jesus that was shed when he was crucified on a cross. Some Christian denominations partake of the Eucharist/Holy Communion/Lord's Supper every Sunday during worship (Roman Catholics, Orthodox, and some Protestants). Others (various Protestant denominations) "celebrate" it once a month or even less frequently.

Clergy: Clergy is the term used for ordained Christian religious leaders (referred to as "priests" in the Roman Catholic, Orthodox, and Episcopalian denomination within Protestantism; all other Protestant clergy are usually called "ministers"). Priest are often called "Father" (then the priest's first or last name). Ministers are called Reverend (then the minister's first or last name). While there are some Protestant churches that are considered "non-denominational," most ordained Christian clergy must complete Master's level of education before one can be ordained. Roman Catholicism, Orthodox Christianity, and a few Protestant denominations do not ordain women, though many Protestant denominations do.

Weekly Worship: *(known as the "Mass" for Roman Catholics and the "Divine Liturgy" for Orthodox Christians, and the "Worship Service" among most Protestants)*

Begins: Usually Sunday mornings (the day of the Resurrection of Jesus) but for Roman Catholics, it could also be Saturday evening. Some congregations today are experimenting with offering worship on other days and at other times.

Ends: One to two hours after it begins for Protestants and Roman Catholics. Orthodox Sunday liturgical services can last for several hours.

Purpose: To gather in community; to give honor and glory to God through prayer and praise; to be fed by the holy scriptures found in the Bible; to learn about Christian discipleship; to be nurtured and strengthened for the work of love in the world.

Theological Emphases: God, Jesus, and the Holy Spirit – the Trinity; sin and salvation; the nature of the church; cost of discipleship; mission to the world.

Important Texts: Any text from the Bible.

Primary Symbols: Cross (representing Jesus' death and resurrection), dove (representing the Holy Spirit), lit candles representing Jesus as the light of the world; white, gold, purple, green and red (and sometimes blue) colors representing the various seasons of the Christian Year.

Liturgical Furniture: An altar/table is used for the sacrament of the Eucharist/Holy Communion, a baptismal font or baptistery is used for the sacrament of Baptism, pulpit is used for preaching, and a lectern (if one is present) is used for the reading of scripture and other parts of the worship service.

Preaching: A sermon or homily is usually preached every week.

Primary Symbolic Acts: Sacrament of the Eucharist/Holy Communion (weekly in Roman Catholic, Orthodox, and some Protestant congregations; monthly or quarterly in most Protestant churches), sacrament of Baptism, prayer, and singing praises to God.

Common Elements:

Prayers (of Thanksgiving, of Confession, of Intercession); Lord's Prayer

Creed (often the Nicene Creed or the Apostle's Creed)

Chanting or singing of hymns and songs by congregation and/or choir or "praise team" accompanied by an organ, piano, or "praise band". In some Orthodox churches and a couple minor denominations in Protestant Christianity, no instruments are allowed. In other Orthodox churches, particular instruments may be used. For example, the Coptic Church makes use of the cymbals and triangle to maintain the rhythm of the hymn.

Reading of Scripture

Sermon/Homily

Eucharist/Holy Communion/Lord's Supper

Responses to the Word read in scripture and preached

Offering of one's resources (time, talents, money)

Closing Benediction (blessing)

Summary of the Christian Year:

The historical story or metanarrative that runs throughout the Christian Yearly Calendar finds its sources in the New Testament of the Christian Bible, particularly in the four Gospels: the Gospel of Matthew, the Gospel of Mark, the Gospel of Luke, and the Gospel of John. The Christian ritual calendar helps Christians stay rooted in the one they recognize as incarnating the very essence of God: Jesus of Nazareth, who is often called the Christ.

The Christian Narrative:

The Christian Year begins with **Advent,** a period of preparation four Sundays prior to December 25 which is the day we celebrate the birth of Jesus, **Christmas**. Christmas is more than just a day however, it is also a season of 12 days culminating on the **Day of Epiphany** when the uniqueness of Jesus is made manifest to others. **Ordinary Time after the Epiphany** depicts the life and ministry of Jesus as Christians come to know just who Jesus is. Texts tell the story of Jesus' baptism, miracles, healings, teachings, and unique nature as the one chosen by God as the beloved son of God. **Lent** is another preparation period of introspection, repentance and self-sacrifice as we approach the time of Jesus' death. The last week of Jesus' life is known as **Holy Week** which encompasses the Triduum, the final three days: **Maundy** or **Holy** Thursday in which Jesus gathered for a last supper with his disciples and instituted the practice of the Eucharist or Holy Communion; Good **Friday**, the day Jesus was crucified on a cross and died; and **Easter Saturday or Holy Saturday** when we continue to mourn the death of Jesus yet await with hopeful anticipation his resurrection from the dead on **Easter Sunday.** Easter is also not limited to one day but is a 50 day period in which the texts retell Jesus' resurrection appearances to his disciples and his final ascension into heaven. The **Great 50 Days of the Easter Season** culminate in the **Day of Pentecost**, when God's gift of the Holy Spirit descends upon the people gathered. This is considered to be the birth of the Christian church.

This period of "narrative time" when we retell the life of Jesus and the birth of the church begins late November/early December (the beginning of Advent) and continues through until May/June (the Day of Pentecost). The timing is totally dependent on when the day of Easter falls each year (Easter Sunday is the Sunday on or after the first full moon on or after the Spring Equinox).

After we re-member and re-live the life and death and resurrection of Jesus, there then follows a time (about 6 months) of deepening our knowledge of the teachings of Jesus, continued growth in what it means to live as a disciple of Jesus, struggling with what the nature of the church is/should be today in relationship to believers and to the world at large (termed "ecclesiology"), and discerning how we can best be in ministry with others (termed "missiology"). Once we have re-heard the story of Jesus, we are called once again to respond to this good news as faithful followers of Jesus.

The scripture texts that support the Christian Year are organized in a "lectionary" which usually assigns 4 texts or readings (several, usually consecutive, verses called a pericope) for each Sunday and extra holy days in the life of the church: one pericope from the Hebrew Bible/Old Testament (except during the season of Easter when readings are from the book of Acts), one from the book of Psalms (also found in the Hebrew Bible/Old Testament), one from the Gospels, and one from the Epistles (letters written by early disciples to the new Christian churches). While there are differences in the lectionaries used by Orthodox Christians, the Roman Catholic lectionary, and the Revised Common Lectionary (used by most Protestant Christians, if the church uses a lectionary at all), during the time from Advent to Pentecost, the readings are remarkably similar. The "Important Texts" identified in this book are the texts associated with the occasion/story and are from the Revised Common Lectionary.

Christians speak of important periods in their year as "seasons": the "season" of Advent or the "season" of Lent or the Easter "season". Seasons (longer periods of time) are the context in which major holidays occur. The two most important days for all Christians are Easter Sunday (celebrating the resurrection of Jesus from the dead) and Christmas Day (which honors the birth of Jesus). Seasons often begin and end with important days in the life of the church: The Christmas Season begins with Christmas Eve and ends with the Day of Epiphany; the season of Lent begins with Ash Wednesday and ends with Good Friday; Easter Sunday begins the Easter season which ends 50 days later on the Day of Pentecost.

These "seasons" are grouped into two major "cycles" in the Christian Year: the Easter Cycle and the Christmas Cycle". In between the two major cycles are periods of "Ordinary Time" which does not mean these are dull or unimportant times. The term "Ordinary Time" derives from the way we count the weeks with ordinal numbers: i.e.: "the *fifth* Sunday after the Epiphany" or "the *twenty-seventh* Sunday after Pentecost". While the Easter Cycle historically developed first, our Christian Year begins with the Christmas Cycle on the first Sunday of the season of Advent.

CHRISTMAS CYCLE
Based on a solar calendar with a set date for Christmas Day – December 25th

November/December
Advent: *Means "Coming"*

Begins: Begins 4 Sundays before December 25th. Advent can last from 22-28 days depending on what day of the week the 25th fall. For Orthodox Christians that follow the Gregorian calendar, Advent will begin 40 days prior to Dec. 25th. For Eastern Orthodox Christians who follow the Julian calendar, Advent will begin 43 days prior to January 6th,(January 5th for the Armenian Church).

Ends: On the evening of December 24th with Christmas Eve worship services. For Orthodox Christians following the Julian calendar, Advent ends on the eve of January 6th/7th (January 5th/6th for the Armenian Church).

Purpose: A season of preparation for the celebration of the birthday of Jesus.

Theological Emphasis: The beginning of Advent is when "time meets". The year has come full circle and in that moment, the end of the one previous year culminates in anticipating a future time when the reign of God (Kingdom of God) will come on earth. For some Christians, it is our calling to help bring this Kingdom of God to earth in our lifetime. This Kingdom is not a political one but one of justice, love, and peace. For other Christians, the future reign of God is when Jesus will come to earth again – the "second coming". This future end time is called "eschatology" (the study of the end of times) and focuses on repentance in readying our hearts and resolve to follow Jesus and do actions of justice to foster the Kingdom of God on earth now. In that moment when "time meets," we also begin a new year remembering the birth, life, ministry, death and resurrection of Jesus and the movement of Jesus' disciples to form the early Christian church. It's a time of anticipating the birth of Jesus – "Emmanuel" – God with us.

Important Texts: In the early part of Advent, texts from the gospels tell the story of John the Baptist's preaching on repentance and preparing oneself for the coming of Jesus (Mt. 3:1-12, 11:2-11, 24:36-44; Mk. 1:1-8, 13:24-37; Lk. 1:68-79, 3:1-6, 21:25-36; Jn. 1:6-8, 19-28). In the latter part of Advent, texts tell the story of The Annunciation (when the angel proclaimed to Mary that she would give birth to God's son – Lk.1:26-38), Joseph's response (Mt. 1:18-25), The Visitation (Mary's visit with her cousin Elizabeth who is the mother of John the Baptist – Lk. 1:39-45), and Mary's song of praise, "The Magnificat" (Lk.1:47-55).

Preaching: While preaching is a regular component of almost every Sunday worship service, during the latter part of the season of Advent, in Protestant congregations, the sermon may be substituted for a service of "Lessons and Carols" (readings from the Bible and hymns/songs) or a dramatic/musical portrayal of the Christmas story by the children or adults.

Moods: Preparation of hearts and homes for the arrival of the divine into the world and into our lives. The season begins with a time of self-inventory and repentance (heightened by the biblical readings) but then shifts to a heightened sense of anticipation as Christmas Eve draws near.

Primary Symbols: The symbolic color for Advent is purple or royal blue.

Advent Wreath (used in worship and in homes): The Advent Wreath is a large wreath of evergreens placed on a table, a stand or the altar with 5 candles positioned within the wreath. One white candle, called the "Christ candle," is placed in the center of the wreath and stands a little taller than the other four candles which are either all purple (a more recent trend is to use bright blue), or three purple and one rose/pink candle. One candle is lit the first Sunday of Advent, then two candles the next week, three the next, etc. The center "Christ Candle" is lit on Christmas Eve. If a rose/pink candle is used, it is lit on the third Sunday which is called Gaudete Sunday (meaning "rejoice"). A reading accompanies the lighting of the candle each week. Some churches will give a name to each candle that helps the congregation mark the movement during Advent: "candle of hope, love, joy, and peace" or "the candle of John the Baptist, Joseph, Mary, the angels". The light of the candles symbolizes Jesus as the light of the world, a theme emphasized in Advent.

Crismon Tree (sometimes used in worship or other spaces in the church – classroom, narthex (foyer), fellowship hall): The Crismon Tree looks like a Christmas Tree but the ornaments on the tree are only white and gold (the liturgical colors for Christmas) and each ornament is a a symbol associated with Jesus (i.e.: cross, lamb, star) or a "monogram" of the names used for Jesus (i.e: IXTHUS – a Greek word meaning "fish" that was used as an acrostic with each letter representing the first of each word in the Greek phrase "Jesus Christ, God's Son, Savior"; Chi Rho – the first two Greek Letters for the word "Christ" - XRISTOS).

Primary Symbolic Acts: Lighting of the Advent Wreath every Sunday for the four Sundays leading up to Christmas Eve.

Required, Recommended or Optional: Adherence to the season of Advent is required for Roman Catholic and Orthodox Christians (known as Nativity). It is recommended by mainline Protestant denominations (required by the Episcopal Church and the Evangelical Lutheran Church in America). For most other Protestant denominations, the season of Advent is optional.

Common Customs:

Hanging of the Greens: decorating the worship area of the church (the sanctuary) with evergreen garlands and trees (symbolizing everlasting life), lights (representing Jesus as the light of the world), wreaths (circle representing eternity), stars, (a star pointed the way for shepherds to find their way to Jesus' birthplace), poinsettias (see below for significance).

Christmas Caroling: Groups of people will sing Christmas hymns to folks in a variety of settings.

Poinsettias: The poinsettia is also called the "Flores de Noche Buena/Flowers of the Holy Night" because of a Mexican legend that tells of a poor young girl who had nothing to give to the baby Jesus on Christmas Eve. On her way to church, she picked some green leaves and laid them at the feet of the statue of Jesus in the Manger scene where they turned into a beautiful red flower that resembled the star that shone over the manger to guide the way of the shepherds and magi (wise men) to Jesus.

Saint Nicholas or Santa Claus: St. Nicholas (bishop of the church in the 4th c.) was known for his care for the poor. Saint Nicholas (often called Santa Claus) brings gifts on Christmas Eve.

Lighting homes: Stringing lights on the outside of houses, putting candles in the windows inside signifies the light of Christ coming into the world.

Manger scenes: Manger scenes depict the baby Jesus lying in a manger surrounded by Mary (mother of Jesus) and Joseph (Mary's husband), animals (usually sheep), three magi (wise men) offering gifts to Jesus, angels (proclaiming the good news of Jesus' birth), and star (which led people to the stable where Jesus was born). While most are replicas of this "scene" of the birth of Jesus, there are some churches that will have a "live manger scene" with people and live animals re-enacting this event.

Advent Calendar: Stores may sell chocolate "Advent" calendars – a chocolate for each day to count down to Christmas – but they always begin with Dec. 1 when in reality, Advent can range from 22-28 days.

Fasting/Feasting Practices: Any fasting done during Advent is up to the individual Christian. Advent tends to be a time of parties in the North American culture.

Foods:

Candy Canes: Represent the shepherd's staff. Jesus is known as the Good Shepherd and shepherds were the first to hear of Jesus' birth.

Christmas Cookies: Represent the sweetness of the Christian life, these cookies are often cut in shapes symbolic of Christmas (stars, circles, trees). These cookies are made and shared with family and friends or given as gifts.

Additional Worship/Prayer/Ritual Services or Special Focus for Regular Weekly Worship/Prayer:

Las Posadas: In Mexican, Mexican-American and some other Latin American cultures, there is a 9 day "Service of Shelter for the Holy Family". Beginning on Dec. 16 and continuing through Dec. 24, congregants visit a different home each night re-enacting the time when Mary and Joseph were seeking shelter for the birth of Jesus.

Christmas Day: *"Christmas" comes from "Christ's mass". "Mass is a Roman Catholic term for the worship service where the Eucharist is celebrated.*

Note: Contrary to media and commercial advertising, the Christmas Season does not officially start in the church until Dec. 24th, Christmas Eve (for Roman Catholic and Protestant Christians; January 6th or 7th for Orthodox Christians following the Julian calendar).

Begins: The evening of Dec. 24th for Roman Catholic and Protestant Christians; January 5th (for the Armenian

Church), January 6th/7th for Orthodox Christians who base their dates on the older Julian calendar.

Ends: The Christmas Season lasts for 12 days and ends on January 6th, the Day of Epiphany which culminates the entire Christmas Cycle or January 19th/20th for Orthodox Christians on the Julian calendar.

Purpose: Celebrates the birth of Jesus.

Theological Emphasis: Incarnation – a physical presence of the divine among us.

Important Texts: Luke 2: 1-20 (the Christmas story), Jn. 1:1-4 (speaks of the Word of God becoming flesh and living among us – incarnation).

Preaching: The services will usually include preaching.

Moods: Very joyous!

Primary Symbols: The symbolic color for Christmas is white. All the decorations from Advent are still present (evergreens, lights, tree, poinsettias, stars, manger scenes).

Primary Symbolic Acts: Lighting of the center white Christ Candle on the Advent Wreath.

Required, Recommended or Optional: All churches would celebrate the Day of Christmas either on Christmas Eve or Christmas Day (Dec. 25th) or both. Even nominal Christians will often attend a worship service on Christmas Eve or day.

Restrictions: If at all possible, people will not work on Christmas Eve or Christmas Day.

Common Customs:

Visit from St. Nick: Especially in homes with children, there is often a "visit from Saint Nicolas/Santa Claus" on Christmas Eve who leaves gifts under a decorated Christmas tree.

Exchanging gifts: People exchange gifts with family, friends, co-workers. Some open gifts on Christmas Eve, others wait until Christmas Day.

Charity: Christians will give gifts and food to those who are in need.

Fasting/Feasting Practices: Christmas Eve and Christmas Day are times of feasting in the home or in the home of family/friends.

Foods: Foods common to Advent are also eaten on Christmas Eve/Day (cookies, candy canes). In the United States, turkey or ham are commonly served meats for Christmas dinner.

Additional Worship/Prayer/Ritual Services or Special Focus for Regular Weekly Worship/Prayer:

Christmas Eve Services: Most Christian churches will have a service on Christmas Eve. Some churches will have an early worship service geared toward children (around 7 or 8 pm) while others will wait until 11:00 pm or midnight (the Midnight Mass) to have their Christmas Eve worship service. Many will offer two or more services on Christmas Eve geared to different populations (more informal and child friendly for families; more formal for adults) and to accommodate the number of people who will attend. The story of the birth of Jesus will be retold.

Candlelight Services: In many Christmas Eve Services, the worship leaders will light a candle from the center white candle of the Advent Wreath, pass that light to the candles held by ushers who will then pass the light to the candles held by all members of the congregation. Done at the end of the worship service, many congregations will sing "Silent Night, Holy Night" during the candle lighting.

Christmas Day: Some congregations will also have a worship service on Christmas morning. For most Christians, the rest of Christmas Day takes place in a home with a large meal and the exchanging of gifts (except for some denominations and Christian cultures who exchange gifts on Jan. 6 – the Day of Epiphany).

Christmas Season: *The remainder of the Christmas season is a time of joy and rest. Many will have time off from work and/or school. There are no additional special services related to Christmas.*

Begins: Eve of December 24th

Ends: January 6 – Day of Epiphany

Important Texts: The Sunday service(s) in this season deals with the Massacre of the Innocents (when Herod ordered all baby boys killed in hopes of killing Jesus – Mt. 2:13-23) and Mary and Joseph's Flight to Egypt with baby Jesus, the Presentation of the infant Jesus in the Temple (where Jesus was proclaimed as a light to the nations – Lk. 2:22-40), and the boy Jesus talking with the rabbis in the Temple (Lk. 2:41-52).

Civic New Year's Eve: Some congregations will have a worship service on New Year's Eve – Dec. 31.

January

Day of Epiphany: *Epiphany means "Manifestation" and is the culmination of the Christmas Cycle*

Begins: January 6th. For those churches that don't have separate worship services during the week, Epiphany can be celebrated in worship the Sunday before or after January 6th. For Orthodox Christians, it is usually January 18th.

Purpose: There are 3 "manifestations" of Jesus associated with the Epiphany:

The visit of the Three Magi (also called Three Wise Men or Three Kings) who followed a star from foreign lands and brought gifts appropriate for a king (gold, silver, and myrrh) to the baby Jesus and were the first Gentiles to pay homage to Jesus. The baptism of Jesus where the Holy Spirit descended upon Jesus in the form of a dove and a voice from heaven proclaimed Jesus as God's beloved son.

The Miracle at Cana where Jesus performed his first miracle by turning vats of water into wine at a wedding feast.

Different denominations/congregations may emphasize one of these "manifestations" of Jesus over the others on this day. Each highlights the uniqueness of Jesus for our world that Christians came to name as the divine presence on earth.

Theological Emphasis: Christology – the study of who Jesus is.

Important Texts: The story of the Three Magi (Mt. 2:1-12), the Baptism of Jesus (Mt. 3:13-17, Mk. 1:4-11, Lk. 3:15-17).

Preaching: Yes.

Moods: Joyous!

Primary Symbols:

Symbolic Color: The color for Christmas season is white or white with gold.

Symbols: stars, a manger scene with the Magi (three Wise Men), the gifts of the Magi (gold, frankincense, and myrrh) or water (primary symbol of baptism) depending on which episode in the life of Jesus is emphasized.

Special Foods: Will vary from culture to culture.

ORDINARY TIME
(between Epiphany and Lent)

January/February
Ordinary Time after the Epiphany: *Ordinary Time is the term used when the Sundays are counted by ordinal numbers. In this season between the Christmas Cycle and the Easter Cycle, Sundays would be counted as the "first Sunday after the Epiphany, second Sunday after the Epiphany, etc.*

Begins: After the Day of Epiphany

Ends: The day before the season of Lent (Shrove Tuesday, the day before Ash Wednesday for Roman Catholics and some Protestant Christians).

Purpose: To learn about the life and ministry of Jesus.

Theological Emphasis: Christology. Who is Jesus? Jesus is the one sent by God, the Son of God, miracle worker, teacher, preacher, healer.

Important Texts: Gospel texts depict who Jesus is: Jesus' first miracle at the Wedding in Cana (Jn. 2:1-11), Jesus calling the first disciples to follow him (Mt. 4:12-23; Mk. 1:14-20, 2:13-22; Lk. 5:1-11), the teachings of Jesus (Mt. 5:1-48, 6:24-34; Lk.4:14-30, 6:17-49), stories where Jesus heals someone (Mk. 1:21-45, 2: 1-12,), miracles of Jesus (Lk. 5:1-11, Jn. 2:1-11), and metaphors for Jesus such as Light of the World (Mt. 5:13-20), salt of the earth (Mt. 5:13-20), Lamb of God (Jn. 1:29-42), physician (Mk. 2:13-22), and teacher/preacher (Mk. 1:21-39).

Moods: A time of learning/remembering the teachings and actions of Jesus.

Primary Symbols: The symbolic   for Ordinary Time is green.

Common Customs:

Shrove Tuesday or Fat Tuesday (Mardi Gras) for Roman Catholic and some Protestant churches: The very last night of this season and the night before the season of Lent begins is known as Shrove Tuesday or Fat Tuesday (Mardi Gras in French). It is also known as "Carnival" which means "farewell to the flesh". The word "shrove" comes from "shrive" which meant confessing one's sins, receiving absolution and repenting. Since Lent begins a time of sacrifice, fasting, and self-denial, Shrove Tuesday was a time to remove all fats from one's home and prepare one's life (in body, mind, and spirit) to faithfully enter the 40 days of Lent. A British practice was to make pancakes from all the fats (oil, milk, eggs) in the house. Many churches will have pancake dinners on Shrove Tuesday because of this tradition. However, Shrove Tuesday took on a party atmosphere in some cultures and is now more popularly known as Mardi Gras or Carnival as people feast and party one last time before the season of Lent begins.

February 2: Various occasions are marked on this day. It is known as Candlemas (the Blessing of the candles used in the worship throughout the year), The Purification of the Blessed Virgin (the 40th day after the birth of Jesus), and the Feast of the Presentation of Jesus in the Temple.

Additional Worship/Prayer/Ritual Services or Special Focus for Regular Weekly Worship/Prayer:

Baptism of Jesus Sunday: Baptism is the initiation rite of all Christians.

Begins/Ends: The first Sunday after the Epiphany (Jan. 6).

Purpose: The first Sunday after the Epiphany remembers Jesus' baptism (when Jesus was baptized in the Jordan river by John and the spirit of God descended in the form of a dove and the voice of God proclaimed Jesus as God's beloved son). This Sunday service encourages us to remember our own baptism and to recommit ourselves to our baptismal vows.

Theological Emphasis: The meaning of baptism and Christian initiation. In baptism, individuals profess faith in Jesus Christ or the parents of infants profess their faith and promise to raise the child in the Christian church until the child is old enough to publicly affirm this faith at a service of "Confirmation" (usually around age 12).

Important Texts: The stories of the Baptism of Jesus (Mt. 3:13-17, Mk. 1:4-11, Lk. 3:15-17, 21-22).

Moods: A time to remember the vows we took at our baptism or confirmation. Personal recommitment to follow the way of Jesus.

Primary Symbols: Water.

Primary Symbolic Acts: In many congregations, the Baptism of Jesus Sunday is a time for new baptisms. It is also a time for church members (the already baptized) to renew their baptismal vows. While baptism once in a person's life is all that is necessary, there are symbolic acts of baptismal renewal that may take place on this Sunday. The leaves of a branch may be dipped in water and flung/sprinkled across the heads of the people as the minister says: "Remember your baptism". Or, members of the congregation may walk to the baptismal font or large bowls of water, dip their thumb in the water, and mark the sign of the cross on their forehead.

Fasting/Feasting Practices: If persons are newly baptized that day, there may be a celebration reception with food following the worship service.

Transfiguration Sunday:

Begins/Ends: The Sunday before Ash Wednesday.

Purpose: The last Sunday after the Epiphany remembers the event in Jesus' life when, up on a mountaintop, the figures of Moses and Elijah appeared and the voice of God came from a cloud proclaiming once again that Jesus was God's beloved son.

Theological Emphasis: Jesus as the beloved child of God.

Important Texts: Stories of the Transfiguration of Jesus (Mt. 17:1-9, Mk. 9:2-9, Lk. 9:28-43).

EASTER CYCLE

Based on a lunar calendar with the date of Easter changing based on the spring equinox and the full moon. Easter for some Orthodox branches is rooted in the Julian calendar.

February/March

Lent: *comes from the word "lencten" which means Spring*

Begins: Ash Wednesday (46 days before Easter – 40 days of Lent plus 6 Sundays when fasting is not permitted since every Sunday is a "little Easter") for Roman Catholics and those Protestants who observe Lent. Since the date of Easter is based on the lunar calendar (the Sunday on or after the first full moon on or after the Spring Equinox), the date of Easter changes each year which means the date of Ash Wednesday also changes each year. For Orthodox Christians, Lent begins 55 days before Easter.

Ends: Easter Eve or sunrise on Easter morning.

Purpose: Historically it began as a period of fasting and preparation for baptism by new converts to Christianity. Today it is a time of penance and preparation for all Christians as we approach the time in the Christian Year when we remember Jesus' crucifixion and death.

Theological Emphasis: Human capacity for sin and evil; the forgiveness that is possible for those who repent of their sins; the opportunity to repent and recommit ourselves to faithful discipleship following God's will for our lives regardless of the cost of this faithfulness.

Important Texts: The Season of Lent begins with Jesus going out into the wilderness for 40 days where he is tempted by earthly aspirations and rejects them all to follow God's will for his life (Mt. 4:1-11; Mk. 1:9-15; Lk. 4:1-13). Then Gospel texts deal with Jesus' teachings about sin and forgiveness (Luke 15:1-3, 11-32; Jn. 9:1-41) and the cost of discipleship (Mk. 8:31-38; Lk. 13:1-9; Jn. 2:13-22, 3:1-21, 4:5-42, 12:20-33). Later in Lent, texts predict Jesus' impending death (Lk. 13:31-35; Jn. 12:1-8) and foreshadow life beyond the grave in the story of the Raising of Lazarus from the dead (Jn. 11:1-45).

Moods: Quiet introspection; a time of self-inventory and repentance; focus on our complicity with sin and evil in our families and communities; contemplation on the sacrifices we can make to bring peace and hope into oppressive contexts where suffering reigns.

Primary Symbols: The symbolic color for Lent is purple.

Common Customs: Self-denial/self-sacrifice and discipline – giving up something for Lent or taking on a commitment (something that would require sacrificing one's time and/or resources) for justice work in the world.

Fasting/Feasting Practices: Lent is traditionally a time of fasting. Some fast on certain days of the week (Fridays), others fast from eating meat, others fast from eating chocolate or other forms of sweets. The question posed is "What are you 'giving up' for Lent?" During this time of Lent we focus on the sacrifice of Jesus on the cross so we are encouraged to find something that we consider a "sacrifice" to offer in return. Fasting is one practice. Others will "sacrifice" time or money in solidarity with causes of justice in our world.

Special Foods: Lent is more a time when we focus on what *not* to eat rather than what do eat.

Additional Worship/Prayer/Ritual Services or Special Focus for Regular Weekly Worship/Prayer:

Ash Wednesday (not observed by many Protestant Christians and all Orthodox Christians):

Begins/Ends: The 46th day before the Protestant and Roman Catholic Easter date.

Purpose: Begins the season of Lent reminding us of our mortality and our need to confess our sins and put ourselves right with God.

Theological Emphasis: Mortality, sin, death in the context of the forgiveness possible through Jesus.

Important Texts: Texts talk of returning to God with all our heart, with fasting and mourning because God is gracious and merciful (Joel 2:1-2, 12-17); practice piety and pray in secret, fast, give alms (Mt. 6:1-6, 16-21); be reconciled to

God (2 Cor. 5:20-6:10); the Psalmists confession of sin and plea for mercy and forgiveness (Ps. 51:1-17).

Moods: Solemn and self-reflective.

Primary Symbols: The symbolic color for Ash Wednesday is purple or gray. Ashes are created by burning the dried palm branches from the previous year's Palm Sunday worship service. In the bible, ashes/dust are associated with our mortality (Ex. 3:19). People also wore sackcloth and ashes when they protested evil acts committed by others (Esther 4:1-2, II Sam. 13:39). Ashes are used in worship for the Imposition of the Ashes portion of the worship service (see below).

Primary Symbolic Acts:

Imposition of the Ashes: The people come forward for the "imposition of the ashes". The minister/priest places his/her thumb in a small bowl of ashes then makes the "sign of the cross" on the person's forehead (draws a small cross with the ashes). The person wears the ashes throughout the day as a reminder of our mortality and willingness to embark on the spiritual disciplines associated with Lent.

Required, Recommended or Optional: All Roman Catholic and some Protestant churches will offer Ash Wednesday services with imposition of ashes.

Fasting from the "Alleluia!": The "Alleluia" is a spoken, often sung part of the weekly worship service that recalls the Day of Resurrection (Easter). Since every Sunday is considered "a little Easter," this "Alleluia" is very appropriate.

But in the season of Lent, it is common in the Roman Catholic and some Protestant churches to "fast" from saying/singing "Alleluia" during the Sundays of Lent. The "Alleluia" returns with great enthusiasm at the Easter celebration.

March/April
Holy Week: *Holy Week is the last week in the Season of Lent, the week before Easter. Churches may have worship services every day during Holy Week, though the last three days are especially important. Oriental Orthodox Christians will have 2-3 services every day, each lasting a few/several hours.*

Begins: Palm Sunday, the Sunday before Easter.

Ends: With either the Easter Vigil on Easter Eve or at sunrise on Easter morning.

Purpose: To remember the last days of Jesus life.

Theological Emphasis: Sin in its various forms: betrayal (Judas Iscariot betrayed Jesus), denial (Peter, one of Jesus' disciples, denied that he even knew Jesus), violence and death (soldiers flogged Jesus, placed a crown of thorns on his head, stabbed him with a spear, death by crucifixion – the form of capital punishment at that time). Many Christians believe that the crucifixion of Jesus is also salvific so the day of Good Friday also deals with forgiveness and atonement.

Important Texts: The Gospel texts cover the episodes in the last days of Jesus' life before his crucifixion. The Palm Sunday story and the Passion Narrative are retold. *(see below for specifics)*

Preaching: It is common for all of these special services to include preaching but this is also a time in the Christian Year when alternative visual, dramatic and ritual symbolic acts hold sway over oral proclamation.

Moods: It begins with Jesus joyously entering the city of Jerusalem with the crowds shouting "Hosanna!" During the week however, the mood takes a drastic turn to one of somber reflection, sadness, and grief as Jesus is betrayed, arrested, denied, tried, flogged, crucified, and buried.

Primary Symbols: The symbolic color for Holy Week is purple with options for grey or black towards the end of the week. (See below for symbols related to specific days).

Restrictions: While there are no work restrictions, many will try to make time to attend a Good Friday service.

Fasting/Feasting Practices: Fasting is common on Good Friday.

Additional Worship/Prayer/Ritual Services or Special Focus for Regular Weekly Worship/Prayer:

Palm Sunday/Passion Sunday:

Begins/Ends: The Sunday before Easter Day; the last Sunday in Lent.

Purpose: To reenact/retell the Palm Sunday story and to prepare us for the Passion Narrative that follows. The Palm Sunday story depicts Jesus riding into Jerusalem with crowds waving branches (usually palms) and shouting "Hosanna! Blessed is he who comes in the name of the Lord!" The Passion narrative reminds us of the multiple ways Jesus was betrayed, denied, beaten, mocked, scorned, tried and crucified.

Theological Emphasis: Sin and evil; violence and injustice; forgiveness from sin and salvation.

Important Texts: Gospel texts portray the Palm Sunday story (Mt. 21:1-11; Mk. 11:1-11; Lk. 19:28-40), and the Passion Narrative – the events leading up to and including Jesus' death by crucifixion (Mt. 26:14-27:66; Mk. 11:1-11, 14:1-15:47; Lk. 19:28-40, 22:14-23:56, Jn. 13:1-17, 31-35, Jn. 18:1-19:42; I Cor. 11:23-26).

Preaching: Usually, although dramatic presentations of the Passion Narrative may substitute for a sermon.

Moods: Of all the days in the Christian Year, Palm/Passion Sunday contains the most drastic mood change. One moment the children are waving palms and shouting "Hosanna!" and the next the people are contemplating the death of Jesus on the cross.

Primary Symbols: Palm branches, a cross.

Primary Symbolic Acts:

Procession: In many congregations, the members of the church gather outside on Palm Sunday and reenact Jesus' procession into Jerusalem by processing into the church waving palm branches and shouting "Hosanna!" If entire congregations don't participate in a procession, children will often reenact this event for us. In the front of the worship space (the chancel part of the sanctuary) is often a cross. The palms will be laid at the foot of the cross.

Dramatic Reading/Reenactment of the Passion Narrative: Since the Passion Narrative is very long and involves many characters and episodes, some congregations will retell this story in a variety of creative ways.

Required, Recommended or Optional: Almost all Christian congregations will observe Palm Sunday in one way or another.

Common Customs:

Making palm crosses. Some will make small crosses out of palm branches for people to wear as a pin or to take home with them as a reminder to be mindful of the events of the upcoming week.

Burning the palm branches. Once the palm branches have dried out, the branches are burned and used as the ashes for next year's Ash Wednesday service.

Triduum: For Roman Catholics, Orthodox Christians, and a few Protestants, the Triduum is one act of worship that lasts for 3 days: Maundy Thursday, Good Friday, and Holy Saturday (Easter Vigil). People don't stay in church for the entirety of the three days but there are services offered on each day culminating in the Easter Vigil on Easter Eve. For the majority of Protestants, instead of Easter celebrations beginning at the Easter Vigil, services will take place at sunrise on Easter morning.

Maundy/Holy Thursday: "Maundy" comes from the Latin word "mandatum," meaning law/commandment.

Begins/Ends: Thursday evening before Easter.

Purpose: Commemorates the last meal Jesus ate with his disciples before his crucifixion (known as the Last Supper), Jesus' act of washing the disciples' feet, and reminds us of the foundational narrative behind the Christian practice of Eucharist (also known as Holy Communion and Lord's Supper).

Theological Emphasis: The sacrament of Communion/Eucharist and how Jesus body/blood/real presence is experienced in eating bread and drinking wine; communion (with one another and with God); servanthood.

Important Texts: The Institution Narrative (the text Christians use as the basis for the sacrament of the Eucharist – I Cor. 11:23-26; Mt. 26:17-30; Mk. 14:22-25; Lk. 22:14-23) and the story of Jesus washing the feet of the disciples (Jn. 13:1-17).

Mood: The somber mood of Holy Week is present this night. Because this is also the night Jesus tells his disciples that one among them will betray him, it is also a reflective mood as we ponder the ways in which we have betrayed one another and have fallen short of being faithful to Jesus.

Primary Symbols: The bread and wine/grape juice of the Eucharist and the basin of water and towel of the footwashing.

Primary Symbolic Acts:

Eucharist/Holy Communion: While participation in the Eucharist is a part of weekly worship in Roman Catholic and Orthodox congregations, it is not so for most Protestant Christians who will celebrate the Eucharist once a month or even once every three months. If a church has a worship service on Maundy Thursday, however, Eucharist will be a central focus. On this night in Jesus' life, he took bread, gave thanks to God, blessed the bread and gave it to his disciples. Likewise he took a cup of wine, gave thanks to God, blessed it and gave it to his disciples to drink. He told his disciples that the broken bread was/was like his body and the wine was/was like his blood. Throughout the centuries Christians have been divided over just what this means which has contributed to the various splits between Christians but Jesus' command to "do this in remembrance of him" has been obeyed.

Footwashing: Following the example of Jesus in John's gospel, congregations may include footwashing on Maundy Thursday. Bowls of water and towels are placed at "stations" around the sanctuary and those who wish to participate go forward and sit in a chair while one of the leaders washes their feet and dries them with the towel. That person may then wash the feet of the next person, etc.

Tenebrae: Tenebrae is the name for a series of biblical texts from the Passion Narrative (usually 16) that are read while light from candles is gradually extinguished until the worship space is darkened. Keeping safety in mind, the overhead lights would be as low as possible. The service begins with all of the candles lit. After each reading, one candle is extinguished until the room is dark. A Tenebrae service may take place on Maundy Thursday or Good Friday.

Stripping the Altar: In preparation for the desolation of the next day, Good Friday, all ornamentation of any kind is removed from the chancel (front raised area of worship space): the bread and wine, altar cloths, vessels, candles and their holders, processional crosses, cloth banners, paraments (cloths decorating the altar and pulpit), etc. When the Stripping of the Altar is complete, the space looks very desolate - an appropriate setting for the Good Friday service.

Draping a black cloth on a large cross: For Holy Week, many congregations will have a large cross visibly present. In Protestant churches that have empty crosses (no body of Christ on them as in the Roman Catholic Church), a black cloth may be draped on the cross.

Required, Recommended or Optional: Worship on Maundy/Holy Thursday would be expected of Roman Catholic and Orthodox Christians. It is strongly recommended for mainline Protestants and optional for other Protestants.

Common Customs:

Seder Meal: In the past 40 years in the United States, there has been a custom of sharing a Seder Meal on Maundy Thursday. The biblical narrative connects the Last Supper with the Jewish Passover (Mt. 26:17; Mk. 14:12; Lk. 22:7-8). As Christians began to understand more about the Passover practices of their Jewish neighbors, some congregations invited rabbis and Jewish laity to teach them the Seder and they participated in a Seder Meal together. However, today, there are some Christian congregations who hold a "Seder Meal" without any attempt to fully understand this important Jewish ritual practice nor is there any goal of developing ongoing interfaith relations with their Jewish neighbors. Therefore the Seder Meal on Maundy Thursday is controversial today.

Fasting/Feasting Practices: Historically Christians would fast on Maundy Thursday with the fast broken by the bread and wine of the Eucharist.

Special Foods: The bread and wine of the Eucharist.

Good Friday: *derived from "God's Friday"*

Begins/Ends: The Friday before Easter.

Purpose: To commemorate the last hours in Jesus' life, his crucifixion and death.

Theological Emphasis: Sin and forgiveness of sins; salvation through Jesus. For some Christians, Good Friday (rather than Easter) is considered the day of atonement.

Important Texts: Peter's denial of Jesus, Judas' betrayal with a kiss, Jesus' arrest, trial, sentence, and crucifixion: Mt. 26:31-27:66; Mk. 14:26-15:47; Lk. 22:31-23:56; Jn. 18:1-19:42.

Preaching: In the United States it is common to have community wide ecumenical Good Friday services where Christians from a variety of denominations will gather to hear sermons on the 7 Last Words of Jesus. These services often take place from twelve noon until three p.m. which is identified in Lk. 23:44 as the time of Jesus' suffering and final death. The "7 Last Words of Jesus" are not found in any one Gospel book but different statements from Jesus found in all four gospels are combined to create this composite of Jesus' last words. Usually a minister/priest from a different denomination takes responsibility to preach on one of the "last words". Each sermon will last about 30 minutes with hymns and prayers in between. People are free to come to one or more of the sermons or stay for the full three hours.

Mood: There are different moods present on this day depending on one's denomination, ethnic cultural background and theology regarding the crucifixion. For much of Christendom, Good Friday is a day of deep sorrow, sadness and grief. However, for those who believe that salvation is located solely in Jesus' death on the cross (as opposed to in the resurrection or in the entirety of Jesus' life, ministry, death and resurrection), Good Friday is seen as a day of celebrating being forgiven for one's sins, the day of atonement.

Primary Symbols:

Symbolic Color(s): The primary symbolic color for Good Friday is black, gray or purple.

Symbols: The cross is the primary symbol of this day.

Primary Symbolic Acts:

Stations of the Cross: Especially in the Roman Catholic tradition, people will pray and meditate at 14 "stations." Each station will be some sort of visual depiction of an episode in Jesus' life just prior to his crucifixion (praying in the Garden of Gethsemene, through his arrest, trial, sentencing, carrying the cross, crucifixion, death, and being laid in the tomb).

Required, Recommended or Optional: Most practicing Christians will observe Good Friday through worship or individual prayer and reflection.

Common Customs:

Good Friday morning prayer breakfast. Some denominations hold a Good Friday morning prayer breakfast. In those denominations influenced by England, hot cross buns are often served at the breakfast. These are a sweet bread, about the size of one's fist, with a cross formed on the top with icing.

Fasting/Feasting Practices: A common day for fasting.

Special Foods: "Hot Cross buns" – warm bread buns with white crosses on the top made out of some sort of icing.

Additional Worship/Prayer/Ritual Services or Special Focus for Regular Weekly Worship/Prayer:

Orthodox Friday Vigil: There will be worship all day on Friday in most Orthodox churches and a vigil of praise on Friday night. Some "praise" texts are only said on this night. Scripture passages from the books of the Hebrew Bible/Old Testament that are not included in the Biblical canon of all Christians (called Deuterocanonical books) are often read this night as well as the entire New Testament Book of Revelation. Some will stay in the church from 10 pm until 5 am Saturday morning. The black cloth of Holy Week will be changed to white for the Good Friday vigil.

Holy Saturday Easter Vigil: Observed primarily by Roman Catholics, though Episcopalians and some Protestant congregations will also begin their Easter celebrations with the Holy Saturday Easter Vigil. For Orthodox Christians who celebrated a vigil on Good Friday, the Holy Saturday Vigil will not be quite as elaborate. For Eastern Orthodox Christians (as well as Roman Catholics and Protestants), the Holy Saturday Vigil is a time of baptism (the Baptismal Vigil).

Begins: After sunset on Easter Eve.

Ends: Most will last at least until midnight Saturday though some will end earlier and others will go into the early morning hours.

Primary Symbols: Fire, Paschal Candle (often two or more feet high), butterfly (symbol of resurrection/transformation).

Primary Symbolic Acts:

Increasing the Light: By the end of Maundy Thursday and Good Friday, light has decreased until darkness has covered the earth (Lk. 23:44). So the Easter Vigil begins in darkness and a new light is created in the form of a fire. From this light, other candles are lit, especially the Paschal Candle, as the light grows in intensity. In some congregations, the people gather outside as a bonfire is lit and then process with lit candles into the darkened sanctuary. As the Paschal candle enters, the overhead lights are also brought up until the people are basking in the light of Christ.

Re-vesting the Altar: For those congregations that "stripped the altar" on Maundy Thursday and removed all objects from the chancel area, those objects need to be returned. They are either present as the Vigil begins or, during the procession, they are brought forward and put back in place. The space shifts from one of desolation to one filled with beauty, color, and joy.

The Story of Salvation History: During the Easter Vigil, texts will be read from the beginning of creation through to the resurrection of Jesus as the fullness of the story of God's saving works in history are retold. In addition to the oral reading of these texts (usually around ten), there are often musical or dramatic responses to the readings.

Baptism: Historically, the new converts to Christianity were baptized at the Easter Vigil so baptism is often a part of Vigil services today. The congregation may also participate in a renewal of their baptismal vows.

Eucharist: It is common for the Vigil to include an Easter Eucharist.

Easter Eve/Day: *The most important day in the Christian year.*

Begins: For Roman Catholic and Protestant Christians, Easter begins at the Easter Vigil on Easter Eve or at sunrise (for most Protestant Christians) on Easter Sunday. The date of Easter is determined by the first Sunday on or after the first full moon on or after the Spring Equinox. All Orthodox Christians who follow the Julian calendar celebrate the same date for Easter which, based on the Spring/Vernal Equinox, occurs about 13 days later than the Gregorian calendar.

Ends: Midnight the same day.

Purpose: To celebrate the resurrection of Jesus from the dead.

Theological Emphasis: Resurrection and new life.

Important Texts: Stories of the resurrection (Mt. 28:1-10, Mk. 16:1-8, Lk. 24:1-12, Jn. 20:1-18).

Preaching: Yes!

Moods: Very joyous!

Primary Symbols: The symbolic color for Easter Day is white (and sometimes gold). Other symbols include the butterfly (symbol of metamorphosis, transformation, and new life from the cocoon), the Paschal Candle, flowers (especially white lilies). Some churches will have a "tomb with the stone rolled away" or a cross draped in white.

Primary Symbolic Acts:

>Paschal Greeting: The worship presider will say (loudly and with great enthusiasm!): "Christ is Risen!!" and the congregation will respond: "Christ is Risen Indeed!"

>Return of the "Alleluia!": For those congregations that "fasted" from singing the "Alleluia!" during the Lenten season, it will be proclaimed/sung during the Easter service.

Required, Recommended or Optional: Every Christian congregation will celebrate Easter. Non-practicing Christians will often attend Easter services.

Restrictions: If at all possible, practicing Christians will not work on Easter Day.

Common Customs:

>Re-Vesting the Altar: If the altar was "stripped" on Maundy Thursday, all vessels, candles, cloths, etc., will be back in place for the full glory of the Easter service.

>Easter lilies: White lilies are often called "Easter lilies". In the same way that many Protestant churches will decorate the worship space with poinsettias at Christmas, churches will decorate the worship space with Easter lilies for the Easter services.

Special Foods: Eating ham on Easter made clear the distinction between Christians and Jews. Greek Orthodox traditions eat lamb on Easter remembering Jesus as the "lamb of God." Hard boiled eggs are dyed red in the Russian Orthodox tradition in honor of a legend surrounding Mary Magdalene where an egg turned red as a miracle confirming her statements about the truth of the resurrection of Jesus during a conversation she had with the emperor of Rome. Coptic Orthodox traditions eat salted mullet

and eggs the following day "Smelling the Breeze" (Sham al-Nessim) which is the beginning of Spring.
Additional Worship/Prayer/Ritual Services or Special Focus for Regular Weekly Worship/Prayer:

> *Easter Sunrise:* Because it was at daybreak that the tomb of Jesus was found empty, those congregations that do not hold an Easter Vigil worship service, will often hold an Easter sunrise service in addition to the regular Sunday morning service(s). The Sunrise service is usually held outdoors (weather permitting) and facing east (when possible) as dawn breaks over the horizon. The service is usually shorter in length and not as elaborate as the one that will be held at the regular worship time. The Easter texts will be read and Easter hymns will be sung; the outdoor setting offers a different beauty and glory than what will be experienced later.

March/April/May
Easter Season - The Great 50 Days:

Begins: Easter Day.

Ends: 50 days later on the Day of Pentecost

Purpose: To testify to the resurrection appearances of Jesus; celebrate new life out of death; learn more about the risen Christ (as opposed to the earthly Jesus).

Theological Emphasis: Resurrection and new life.

Important Texts: The Gospel readings for the Great 50 Days focus on the resurrection appearances of Jesus (Lk. 24:13-48; Jn. 20:19-31, 21:1-19), Jesus' Ascension into heaven (Lk. 24:44-53; Acts 1:1-14), and texts from the Gospel of John that teach us more about who Jesus is and what Jesus wants for his followers (Jn.

10:1-18, 22-30, 13:31-35, 14:15-21, 23-29, 15:1-17, 17:1-11). In the Easter season, lectionary readings from the Acts of the Apostles substitute for the Hebrew bible lesson each week.

Moods: Joyous.

Primary Symbols: The symbolic color for the Great 50 Days of Easter is white (and sometimes gold). Paschal candle continues to be lit during this season.

Additional Worship/Prayer/Ritual Services or Special Focus for Regular Weekly Worship/Prayer:

Ascension Day: Some denominations will have a separate worship service on Ascension Day, the 40th day after Easter which commemorates the day Jesus ascended into heaven.

May/June
Day of Pentecost:

Begins: The 50th day after Easter.

Ends: Midnight the same day.

Purpose: To remember the day when tongues of flames (representing the presence of the Holy Spirit) descended upon the people allowing each person to understand the foreign languages of the others present; to reaffirm the presence and role of the Holy Spirit in our lives; to honor the tradition that designates this day as the birthday of the Church.

Theological Emphasis: Pneumatology (understanding the Holy Spirit).

Important Texts: The story of Pentecost (Acts 2:1-21).

Moods: Celebratory!

Primary Symbols: The symbolic color for Pentecost is red. The dove (a symbol of the Holy Spirit) and flames depicted on cloth paraments and vestments symbolize the tongues of fire that descended on the people at Pentecost.

Primary Symbolic Acts:

Baptism: In addition to Easter and the Baptism of Jesus Sunday, Pentecost is the other most common day in the life of the church for baptisms to take place.

Required, Recommended or Optional: All Roman Catholic and Orthodox Christians as well as many Protestant congregations will observe the Day of Pentecost.

Additional Worship/Prayer/Ritual Services or Special Focus for Regular Weekly Worship/Prayer:

Multiple Languages: Since the Pentecost text (Acts 2:1-21) tells the story of the good news of Jesus being proclaimed in a multitude of languages and the Holy Spirit gave people the ability to understand these various "tongues," the Day of Pentecost is a time when the text (or other parts of the worship service) may be conducted in a variety of languages.

ORDINARY TIME
(between Pentecost and Advent)

May – November

Ordinary Time after Pentecost:

Ordinary Time is the term used when the Sundays are counted by ordinal numbers. In this season between the Easter Cycle and the Christmas Cycle, Sundays would be counted as the "First Sunday after Pentecost," "Second Sunday after the Pentecost," etc.

Begins: The day after Pentecost. The first Sunday is Trinity Sunday.

Ends: About 6 months later on the day before the first Sunday of Advent. The last Sunday is Christ the King Sunday.

Purpose: To continue learning about the life and ministry of Jesus; to learn about the witness of the early disciples who started the Christian church; to reflect on the role of the church and its mission in today's world.

Theological Emphasis: Missiology (mission of the church), ecclesiology (role of the church), discipleship.

Important Texts: Because the Roman Catholic and Orthodox bibles contain additional books, readings from those texts are often included in this time of the Christian Year. In the three-year Revised Common Lectionary, the next six months continue to tell the story of salvation history, the ministry of Jesus, and the issues facing the followers of Jesus as they establish churches throughout the region.

Year A:

   Hebrew Bible texts tell the stories of the great ancestors of the faith

   Epistle texts include letters written to churches in Rome, Philippi, and Thessalonica.

   Gospel texts follow the life of Jesus as told by the Gospel of Matthew.

Year B:

   Hebrew Bible texts trace the rise of the monarchy in Israel and documents the stories of the kings.

   Epistle texts include letters written to churches in Corinth, Ephesus, as well as a general letter written to numerous churches (book of James), and a sermon style treatise (rather than a letter) written to a church in Rome (book of Hebrews).

   Gospel texts follow the life of Jesus as told by the Gospel of Mark.

Year C:

Hebrew Bible texts teaches about the Prophets.

Epistle texts include more portions from the book of Hebrews, letters written to churches in Galatia, Colossae, and Thessalonica as well as two letters written to individuals (Philemon and Timothy).

Gospel texts follow the life of Jesus as told by the Gospel of Luke.

Moods: Except for the specific days/Sundays listed below, Ordinary Time doesn't have the great celebrations or the periods of solemn reflection found in other seasons of the Christian Year.

Primary Symbols: The symbolic color for Ordinary Time is green, representative of growth in the faith.

Additional Worship/Prayer/Ritual Services or Special Focus for Regular Weekly Worship/Prayer:

Trinity Sunday: *(for Roman Catholic and some Protestant congregations)*

Begins/Ends: The first Sunday after the day of Pentecost. (The first Sunday after Pentecost in Orthodox contexts is All Saints Day - see below).

Purpose: Trinity Sunday reiterates the Trinitarian nature of God. The "Trinity" language in Christianity speaks of God as "*one* God in three persons": God, Jesus, and the Holy Spirit. Understanding the uniqueness of the "three persons" and yet keeping these "persons" of God in a unified "oneness" is the focus of this Sunday. It is the basis of the Baptismal formula ("I baptize you in the name of the Father (God), the Son (Jesus), and the Holy Spirit") used as persons become initiated into the Christian religion.

Important Texts: Jesus' commission to the disciples to "Go and make disciples of all nations, baptizing them in the name of the Father and of the Son and of the Holy Spirit" (Mt. 28:16-20); the text that is used most often at the close of Sunday morning worship as a Benediction (a blessing): "The grace of the Lord Jesus Christ, the love of God, and the communion of the Holy Spirit be with all of you." (2 Cor. 13:1-14).

All Saints' Day/All Souls' Day:

Begins/Ends: Nov. 1/Nov. 2. November 1st is All Saints' Day, a time in the church when the officially recognized "saints" within the Roman Catholic Church are celebrated. Nov. 2nd, All Souls' Day, remembers all Christians who have died who lived faithful lives following the teachings of Jesus. Since Protestant churches don't have canonized saints, if they celebrate All Saints'/All Souls' Day at all, on the Sunday closest to Nov. 1, they will combine the purpose of both of these days and remember all the "saints" of the past and those congregational members who have died the past year. For Eastern Orthodox Christians, All Saints' Day is celebrated on the Sunday after Pentecost.

Important Texts: The texts deal with those who have died, the blessings of God (The Beatitudes - Mt. 5:1-11; Lk. 6:20-31), and the reward of the faithful. John's gospel tells the story of the raising of Lazarus from the dead (Jn. 11:32-44).

Moods: All Saints' Day/Sunday has a mixture of mourning and sadness over those who have died, yet joy in the saints who have gone before us and who now rest in the presence of God.

Primary Symbols: The symbolic color for All Saints'/All Souls' Day is white. Other symbols include candles, bells, photographs/icons/pictures of the "saints".

Primary Symbolic Acts:

Tolling of the Bell: The names of those within the congregation who died during the past year may be read followed by the "tolling of a handbell".

Lighting candles: Members of the congregation may come forward and light a candle in honor of the "saints" in their own lives who have died.

Christ the King Sunday:

Begins/Ends: The last Sunday after Pentecost which is also the last Sunday of the Christian Year.

Purpose: This Sunday has varied interpretations throughout Christianity. For some it is the end of the Christian Year and a celebration of the completion of this year. For others it is a recognition that Jesus is not a political king but rather rules in our hearts as we seek to follow his example on the cross – offering forgiveness to those who crucified him, offering salvation to the one crucified next to him, offering forgiveness to us throughout the ages. For others it is a time to focus on a future date when Jesus will return to earth and establish a political reign.

Important Texts: Texts for this Sunday deal with images of kingship associated with Jesus (Mt. 25:31-46; Jn. 18:33-37; Lk. 23:33-43; Rev. 1:4-8).

The Islamic Calendar

Diversity within Islam:
The majority of Muslims identify as a follower of one of two groups within Islam:
Sunni: .9 % of the US population; 87% of the world's Muslim population and Shia about 13%.
Shia: <.3% of the US population; 13% of the world's Muslim population[1].

Celebrated by both Sunnis and Shias, Eid-ul Fitr ("Feast of Breaking the Fast" commemorated at the conclusion of the month of fasting [Ramadan]) and Eid-ul-Adha ("Feast of Sacrifice" to commemorate Abraham's willingness to offer up his son, Ishmael, as a sacrifice), are considered the two most important holy days within the Islamic Calendar. Even nominal Muslims often attend prayer services and other activities related to these two great festivals.

Important Vocabulary:
Allah/God: While many Muslims believe that "Allah" is the proper name and only name that should be used for "God," "Allah" is an Arabic word meaning "the God" (as in the *only* God). It is the same God to whom Jews and Christians pray. Because non-Muslims often associate "Allah" with a different god from the one that Jews and Christians follow,

---

[1] Pew Research: Religion and Public Life Project, data from 2009. http://religions.pewforum.org/affiliations; http://www.pewforum.org/2009/10/07/mapping-the-global-muslim-population/ accessed 10-11-14.

we have chosen to use the English translation of the Arabic term throughout this chapter: "God". Some Muslims prefer to use "Allah" even in translation because it is a gender-neutral term with no plural form.

Ar-Rahman: The All-Merciful. One of the ninety-nine Beautiful Names of God referring to God's boundless, infinite, and all-comprehensive Mercy. This attribute can only be applied to God and no one else. It is also the title of the 55th chapter of the Qur'an.

Muhammad: The last in the chain of Abrahamic prophets sent by God to guide humanity. He was a descendant from the line of Ishmael; the one to whom God revealed the sacred scripture mediated by the Angel Gabriel (*Jibra'il*) that comprise the Qu'ran, which is viewed by Muslims as the perpetual and standing miracle. *Note: It is a matter of respect to say "peace be upon him" every time the name of the Prophet Muhammad is mentioned. Therefore, throughout this chapter you will see (PBUH) as an abbreviation of this phrase after the word Prophet (when it is capitalized) and Muhammad (PBUH).*[1]

Qu'ran: The sacred scripture of Islam that Muslims believe is divine communication and a verbatim speech of God that was gradually revealed to Muhammad (PBUH) over a period of 23 years (610 – 632 CE). It comprises 114 chapters (*surah*) arranged more or less according to length, from the longest to shortest, and about 6,200 verses (*ayah*). It is divided into 30 equal sections (*juz*) to facilitate its recitation over the

---

[1] The formula used by the Shias would add blessings upon the Prophet's immediate family, i.e., "peace and blessings be upon him and his Household."

course of a month, especially during Ramadan. The Qur'an is NOT compiled in the chronological sequence of its revelation and thus understanding the socio-historical context of a particular verse's revelation is vital.

Hadith/Sunnah: Collected sayings, actions, and tacit approval of Muhammad. It is second in authority to the Qu'ran as a source of Islamic law and ethics. There are two parts to the Hadith: the texts or sayings themselves (*matn*) and the chain of transmission of these texts (*isnad*). They were gathered almost two centuries after Muhammad's (PBUH) death and thus contain many fabrications and false reports. As such, there are established guidelines to determine which are considered the most reliable.

Khutbah: Sermon or oration delivered, especially at the weekly midday congregational prayer each Friday and during prayers of the two great festivals mentioned above. It is divided into two parts with a short break in between for individual reflection and prayer.

Minbar: Elevated structure in a mosque from where a sermon (*khutbah*) is delivered.

Imam: Literally, one who stands out in front. Commonly used to refer to a Muslim male who is recognized by the community as someone with religious leadership gifts and skills. It is not an ordained position and while most would have studied in one of the Muslim seminaries around the world, there are no standardized educational requirements. It is also used to denote a person leading a congregational prayer as well as for the founders of the four Sunni schools of thought. However, Shias use the term "Imam" in a technical sense to refer to the Twelve infallible designated successors of the Prophet (PBUH), each one of whom they believe possess temporal and religious authority. The last one, the Mahdi, went into concealment in the tenth century and is to appear at the end of time with Jesus to inaugurate peace and justice on Earth.

Ahl-ul-Kitab: People of the Book. Initially used to designate the Jews and Christians who are recipients of the Hebrew Bible and the New Testament respectively. It was later extended to include Zoroastrians and other faith groups.

Fatihah: "The Opening." The Qur'an's first chapter that is recited twice during each cycle of the daily ritual prayer. It is comparable to the "Lord's Prayer."

Qiblah: The direction toward which Muslims offer their daily prayers. In the mosque, it is generally indicated by an indented niche.

Weekly Prayer – *Yawm-ul-Jum'ah* – the Day of Assembly:

Begins: Friday around mid-day.

Ends: One-half hour to an hour after it begins.

Purpose: To pray together as a community; to give honor and glory to God; to learn about the teachings of Muhammad (PBUH); to be nurtured and strengthened by the Qu'ran and Hadith for faithful daily living.

Theological Emphases: The oneness of God; the revelation of God through the Prophet Muhammad (PBUH); sin and forgiveness; human inter-relations; service to humanity.

Important Texts: Any text from the Qu'ran or Hadith.

Orientation of Prayer Space: People will face the direction of the Ka'bah, the cubical structure in Mecca.

Items to Accompany Prayer: Prayer mats and beads. Shias use an Earth tablet or rock when prostrating because all seven parts of the body should be touching the Earth to exemplify humility in the presence of God.

Preaching: Two sermons (*khutbah*) are delivered by the imam every week with a short pause in between for individual prayer and meditation.

Common Elements:

Call to Prayer (*adhan*) by the *muezzin* (the one who sings/chants the Call to Prayer) from the minaret and facing towards Mecca:

God is most Great (four times)

I bear witness that there is no god but God (twice)

I bear witness that Muhammad is the Messenger of God (twice)

I testify that Ali is the beloved of God and successor to the Messenger of God (twice)[1]

Hasten to prayer (twice)

Hasten to success and prosperity (twice)

Hasten to the best of deeds (twice)[2]

God is most Great (twice)

There is no god but God[3]

2 sermons (khutbah) with a short pause in between them.

2 cycles of prayer (salat)

---

[1] This is customarily added in the Shia *adhan* but is not considered an integral part of the *adhan*.

[2] Shias regard this phrase as an integral part of the *adhan*.

[3] Recited twice by the Shias.

Summary of the Islamic Calendar:

The Islamic Calendar is based on a lunar cycle and counts the years from June 622 CE because it coincides with Muhammad's (PBUH) migration from Mecca to Medina, which was a turning point in Islam's trajectory to becoming a well-established "community" with institutions. This migration is known as the *hijrah*. Because it is a true lunar calendar (no leap month is added periodically to keep festivals occurring during the same time of the year as with the Jewish calendar), the Islamic year is shorter (only 354.37 days rather than 365 days). Islamic months last 29 or 30 days. Festivals listed below occur approximately 11 days earlier than the previous year. The evening of September 11, 2018 will mark the beginning of the Islamic New Year 1440 AH, meaning "anno hegirae", in the year of the Hijra.

The Muslim Narrative:

The Islamic New Year begins with the celebration of **hijrah** on the first of the month of Muharram. **Hijrah** is the name for both the celebration of the New Year and Muhammad's (PBUH) migration from Mecca to Medina which was the beginning of Islam as a "community" of faith. Fleeing persecution, Muhammad (and, over time, most of the Muslims in Mecca) migrated to a welcoming community in Medina.

Shias, on the other hand, inaugurate the New Year in a somber mood for it coincides with the martyrdom of the grandson of the Prophet and the second Shia Imam, Husayn (the son of Ali or the First Imam) on the 10th of Muharram (or Ashura) on the plains of Karbala in Iraq in 680 CE.

Ashura (or the tenth) evokes different memories for Sunni and Shia Muslims. For Sunnis, it is a time to remember God saving the Israelites through the events of the Exodus. For Shias, it is a time of mourning those who were massacred in the Karbala episode, especially Husayn, the grandson of Muhammad (PBUH) and the son of Ali (cousin and son-in-law of the Prophet [PBUH] and the First Shia Imam).

The rest of the Islamic year highlights events and teachings in the life of the Prophet Muhammad (PBUH) and the sources of the 5 Pillars of Islam. After Ashura, *Rabi-ul-Awwal* (third lunar month) celebrates the birth and death dates of the Prophet (PBUH). *Isra* and *Mi'raaj* (Ascension) remembers Muhammad's (PBUH) amazing night journey to Jerusalem and ascension to heaven where he was confirmed as God's choice to be the final prophet. It was on this journey that directives like the five daily prayers (**Salat**), one of the Pillars of Islam, was enshrined for the people. **Fasting** is another Pillar of Islam wherein the devotee is mandated to fast from dawn to dusk during the ninth month (Ramadan) in the lunar calendar. It is a time to detoxify the body and soul from moral and spiritual impurities so one can begin anew. Ramadan also celebrates the Qur'an's revelation to Muhammad (PBUH), advocates the giving of alms (**Zakat** – another Pillar of Islam), and culminates with the "Feast of Breaking the Fast" (*Eid-ul Fitr*), the most important day in the life of the Islamic community.

For those who can physically and financially make the journey, the *Hajj* (pilgrimage to Mecca and another Pillar of Islam) is performed in the last month of the Islamic Calendar. During this ritual, pilgrims re-enact, remember, and re-live the story of Abraham, Hagar, and Ishmael: their faithfulness and ability to resist temptation, their struggle to find water in the desert and God's gracious provisions of an animal for sacrifice and a well for water. Pilgrims also pray at the Ka'bah, the sanctuary dedicated to the worship of God that Muslims believe was built by prophet

Abraham and his son, Ishmael. Muslims stand on the *Day of Arafat* (9th of Dhul Hijjah) experiencing redemption and the presence of God before they offer their own sacrifice to God on the "Feast of Sacrifice" (*Eid al-Adha*), the second most important day for Muslims.

THE ISLAMIC CALENDAR

Muharram (the first month of the Islamic calendar) - means "forbidden" because it is one of the four holy months during which fighting and war are forbidden.

Dawn of Islamic New Year:

Begins/Ends: 1st of Muharram (sunset on the last day of the last month, Dhul-Hijja).

Purpose: Celebrates the New Year for Sunni Muslims and a time of mourning and grief for Shia Muslims due to the martyrdom of the grandson of the Prophet on the tenth of Muharram.

Theological Emphasis: Sunnis: The entire Earth belongs to God. Thus, one can celebrate God's Glory in other places by migrating. Shia: Oppression should not go unanswered.

Moods: Joyous for Sunnis and grief for Shias.

Primary Symbolic Gestures: Shias: Wearing black attire, light beating of the chest, and donating blood.

Required, Recommended or Optional: Recommended

Restrictions: Shias: Celebrating joyous events like marriage or purchasing a new house.

Common Customs: Setting spiritual goals for the upcoming year that will bring us closer to God. Shias: Commitment to stand up for justice and help the oppressed and disenfranchised.

Fasting/Feasting Practices: Shias: Fasting for half a day on Ashura until late afternoon when Husayn was martyred.

Additional Worship/Prayer/Ritual Services or Special Focus for Regular Weekly Worship/Prayer: Shias: Special rituals and supplications will take place on Ashura. They also gather together every night for the first ten nights of Muharram to listen to sermons and participate in rituals of grief.

Lectures/Spiritual Activities: As communities gather to celebrate the New Year, there may be occasions for educational and/or spiritual development.

Ashura:

Begins/Ends: 10th of Muharram (sunset to sunset 9th/10th).

Purpose: Sunnis: Remembers Noah's ark settling on dry ground after the great flood and commemorates the Exodus when the Jews crossed the Red Sea. Shia Muslims (as well as some Sunnis) remember this day as the day of the Karbala massacre wherein Husayn, the grandson of the Prophet, was brutally killed on the plains of Karbala, Iraq along with his male family members and about 100 companions in 680 CE (61 AH).

Theological Emphasis: Stand up for justice.

Important Texts: Books that relate the historical narrative of Karbala.

Moods: Moods are mixed depending on whether one is Shia or Sunni. For the former, it is a solemn and somber day of mourning. In some Sunni observances on this day, the somberness of the occasion will also be recognized.

Primary Symbolic Gestures:

Acts of Mourning: For Shias, shedding of tears, striking one's chest, and other forms of identification with the unjust suffering of Imam

133

Husayn and others killed in the Karbala massacre.

Required, Recommended or Optional: Optional.

Fasting/Feasting Practices: Ashura is a day of fasting focusing on seeking forgiveness of one's sins through repentance and deepening one's spiritual life. Many believe fasting on this day preceded Islam and was borrowed from the Jews who fasted in thanksgiving for the Jews escape from the Egyptians during the Exodus. To distinguish themselves from the Jews, however, instead of one day of fasting, many will fast for the 9 days leading up to the 10th of Muharram as well. A fast on this day is as if one has fasted for a year.

Shias: Fasting for half a day on Ashura until late afternoon when Husayn was martyred.

Safar (second month) – the word Safar is associated with "empty, yellow, whistling of the wind"

Arba'een – 40th Day:

Begins/Ends: 20th of Safar, 40 days after Ashura

Purpose: Observed by Shia Muslims, Arba'een marks the end of the mourning period (40 days) for the martyrdom of Imam Husayn, the grandson of the Prophet Muhammad (PBUH) and his supporters in Karbala. People will also remember the suffering of the women and children in Husayn's household who were chained and taken as prisoners from Iraq to Syria. With millions of people making pilgrimage to the city of Karbala in Iraq, it is one of the largest gatherings on Earth.

Theological Emphasis: Stand up for justice and give a voice to the oppressed and persecuted.

Moods: Sadness.

Primary Symbolic Gestures: Making pilgrimage to Karbala. During the pilgrimage, many will crawl on their hands and knees or fall down and kneel beside the shrines of Husayn, Abbas (Husayn's step brother), and others.

Additional Worship/Prayer/Ritual Services or Special Focus for Regular Weekly Worship/Prayer:

Recitation: Shias: People on pilgrimage (or in their homes if they cannot make the pilgrimage) will recite a special elegy which elaborates on the events that unfolded after the massacre and also a "visitation formula" in which greetings and salutations are sent to the martyrs and a pledge is made to support the cause of justice.

Du'as: Special prayers (du'as) will be offered highlighting Husayn's martyrdom and favor with God.

Rabi'-ul-Awwal (third month) - means "first Spring"

Hijrah – The Migration of Prophet Muhammad (PBUH):

Begins/Ends: Sometime in the early part of Rabi'-ul-Awwal (around the 8th).

Purpose: Commemorates the migration of the Prophet Muhammad (PBUH) from Mecca to Medina in 622 CE, which marks the beginning of Islam as a religious and cultural community. This migration also became the starting point from which the Islamic Calendar eventually began. The year of the migration was later determined to be year 1 in the Islamic calendar – 1 AH.

Moods: Joyous.

Additional Worship/Prayer/Ritual Services or Special Focus for Regular Weekly Worship/Prayer:

Lectures/Spiritual Activities: To remember and honor the Prophet's (PBUH) migration to

Medina, educational opportunities are often available for people to learn about the event and lectures may be given on the reasons why people migrate then and now: seeking freedom of religion, political asylum, fear of torture and persecution, hunger and economic security.

Milad-un Nabi

Begins/Ends: 12th of Rabi'-ul-Awwal (sunset to sunset 11th/12th) for Sunnis; 17th of Rabi'-ul-Awwal (sunset to sunset 16TH/17TH) for Shias.

Purpose: Celebrate Prophet Muhammad's (PBUH) birth.

Theological Emphasis: To follow the example of the Prophet (PBUH).

Moods: Joyous.

Common Customs:

Lectures: Some mosques will offer special lectures that chronicle the life of Prophet Muhammad (PBUH).

Parades: In some Islamic countries, parades are set up to celebrate the Prophet's birthday.

Illumination: Lights in various shapes (i.e.: stars, crescent moon) may decorate buildings and roadways.

Rabi'-uth-Thani (fourth month) - means "second Spring"

Jamad-il-Awwal (fifth month) – the term Jamad-il-Awwal is associated with "first freeze" or "dry" or "first summer"

Jamad-ith-Thani (sixth month) – the term Jamad-ith-Thani is associated with "second freeze" or "dry" or "second summer"

Rajab (seventh month - another holy month where fighting and war is prohibited) - means "to respect"

Isra' & Mi'raj:

Begins/Ends: 27th of Rajab (sunset to sunset 26th/27th).

Purpose: Celebrates Prophet Muhammad's (PBUH) journey to "the farthest Mosque" presumed to be the Temple in Jerusalem and ascension to heaven. Guided by the angel Gabriel and on Buraq, a beast with wings, the Prophet (PBUH) undertook an amazing night journey. "Isra' is the term for the first stage of the night journey where Muhammad (PBUH) traveled to Jerusalem and was in prayer with various prophets. He was offered the choice between a cup of wine or milk and Muhammad's (PBUH) choice of the cup of milk was a sign of the purity of his heart. "Mi'raj" is the term for the second part of his journey – his ascension to the many levels of heaven. As he ascended through the seven levels of heaven, he received confirmation of God's choice of him as God's Prophet from Adam, Yahya (John), son of Zachariah, and Jesus, son of Mary, Moses, Abraham, Joseph, son of Jacob, and others. At the Lote tree of Paradise, which was at the boundary of God's throne, God prescribes 50 daily prayers for Muslims. On the descent down from heaven, Moses encourages Muhammad (PBUH) to negotiate with God for a fewer number of daily prayers. The number was eventually settled at 5 daily prayers which is what continues today as one of the five pillars of Islam. Remembering and reliving this amazing journey through the levels of heaven also reiterates the belief that Muhammad (PBUH) is truly the Messenger of God since so many important figures at each level confirm God's choice of Muhammad (PBUH) as the Prophet. Faith in the oneness of God and the finality of the prophethood of Muhammad (PBUH) is the essence of the first Pillar of Islam – *Shahada* (Dual Testimony of Faith: I testify that there is no god but God and Muhammad is God's servant and Messenger).

Important Texts: Qur'an, 17:1 (i.e., chapter 17 and verse 1).

Preaching: Many imams will dedicate the sermon (*khutbah*) to the topic of Muhammad's (PBUH) journey.

Moods: Awe and gratitude for the gift of the daily prayers.

Common Customs:

School Holiday: In many Muslim cultures, this is a school holiday.

Fasting/Feasting Practices: Should not be a special fast day.

Additional Worship/Prayer/Ritual Services or Special Focus for Regular Weekly Worship/Prayer:

Lectures: In many mosques and Islamic Centers there are special lectures commemorating the event.

Sha'ban (eighth month) - means "to spread and distribute" or "undisturbed increase"

The month of Sha'ban is a time to reflect on one's life and actions; one's faithfulness to God and to prepare oneself spiritually for the upcoming month-long fast of Ramadan.

Mid Shaban:

Begins/Ends: 15th of Sha'ban (sunset to sunset 14th/15th).

Purpose: Shias celebrate the birth of their 12th and final Imam, Muhammad al-Mahdi in Samarra, Iraq in 869 CE. Due to intense persecution of the Shias by the Abbasids, he goes into Minor Occultation (concealment) from 874-941, during which he was accessible to his followers through one of his agents. In 941 his fourth and last agent declared that the Imam had entered the Major Occultation (concealment) and would not be accessible until his return toward the end of time with Jesus Christ in order to inaugurate peace and justice on Earth.

Ramadan (ninth month) - means "parched thirst"

Ramadan:

Begins: 1st of Ramadan (sunset on the last day of the eighth month, Sha'ban).

Ends: 1st of Shawwal when the fast is broken after sunset on the last night of Ramadan at the Eid al-Fitr.

Purpose: Ramadan is a time to begin anew, spiritually and physically. One's spiritual life is deepened through self-discipline and charity to others. Ramadan reconnects the faithful to God and to the Qu'ran. Muslims fast from sunrise to sunset learning self-control and empathy for those in our world who live in perpetual states of hunger. It is a time to detoxify one's body and one's soul through reflecting on God and the many revelations of God. Though fasting may take place at other times of the year, fasting at Ramadan fulfills the fourth Pillar of Islam – *Sawm* (self-purification). Likewise, while giving charity may occur throughout the year, it is during the month of Ramadan that 2.5% of one's capital will be given to charity which fulfills the third Pillar of Islam, *Zakat* (almsgiving).

Theological Emphasis:

Divine textual revelation: The month of Ramadan encourages believers to remember the various revelations of God throughout history that culminate in the Qu'ran: the "suhuf" or "scriptures" revealed to Abraham, the Torah revealed to Moses, the Psalms revealed to David, the New Testament revealed to Jesus, the Qu'ran revealed to Muhammad (PBUH).

Mercy, Forgiveness, Grace: The month of Ramadan is divided into three sections with the first 10 days focused on God's gift of mercy, the middle 10 days focused on God's gift of forgiveness, and the final 10 days focused on God's gift of grace.

Important Texts: Qur'an, 2:183 and 185 and chapter 97.

Moods: Self-reflection, attentiveness to the soul, anticipation of the spiritual journey that accompanies the fast, empathy for the disenfranchised and poor.

Primary Symbolic Gestures:

Standing: People may stand for long hours in prayer during the evenings.

Common Customs:

Zakat: Zakat represents the alms which is customarily offered during the month of Ramadan in thanksgiving for the blessings of this month. 2.5% of one's net worth is given in charity to benefit the needy.

Fasting/Feasting Practices: Fasting takes place from dawn until sunset every day for the entire month: no liquid, no food, no sexual relations. Fasting is an obligation during Ramadan for those who are physically able. Fasting cleanses the body and the soul and is a spiritual discipline that offers the opportunity to make amends for one's sins or neglect of ritual duties and to set new priorities for one's life.

Foods: Meals that are eaten after sunset each day to break the fast are called "Iftar" dinners.

Additional Worship/Prayer/Ritual Services or Special Focus for Regular Weekly Worship/Prayer:

Sunni: Special daily prayers (*salat-ut-tarawih*) are offered every night during this month in which one section of the Qur'an is customarily read.

Shia: One section of the Qur'an is read in a sitting posture along with special supplications for the month.

Reading the Qu'ran: During Ramadan, God's revelation of the Qu'ran to Muhammed (PBUH) is highlighted. Reading the entire Qu'ran during this month adds a special blessing to one's spiritual journey so the Qu'ran has been divided into 30 sections, one for each day of the month.

Lailatul Qadr – Night of Power/Measure/Destiny

Begins/Ends: One of the odd nights of the last 10 days of Ramadan (i.e. the night of the 21st, 23rd, 25th, 27th, or 29th)[1].

Purpose: Celebrates the night the angel Gabriel received the words of the Qu'ran from God and began transmitting it to the Prophet Muhammad (PBUH).

Theological Emphasis: Revelation.

Restrictions: During the last 10 days of Ramadan people are not expected to work. In Muslim countries, there will be time off from work and studies during this time so people can attend to spiritual and ritual activities.

Fasting/Feasting Practices: Since *Lailatul Qadr* takes place in the month of Ramadan, fasting still takes place from dawn until sunset.

Shawwal (tenth month) - means "to be light and vigorous"

---

[1] The Shias add the 19th night as well.

Eid-ul Fitr – "Feast of Breaking the Fast": *Though known as the "minor" Eid, this is the most important festival of the Islamic year!*

Begins: 1st of Shawwal (after sunset on the last day of Ramadan). This is a three day feast and celebration!

Ends: After sunset on the 3rd of Shawwal.

Purpose: Offers thanks to God for the gifts of mercy and forgiveness during this month and the ability to complete the fast. A time to share some of the blessings with the poor and to empathize with their plight. Eid-ul Fitr also celebrates the faithfulness and devotion of all those who fasted the entire month.

Theological Emphasis: Focuses on repentance, mercy and forgiveness of sins; sharing the blessings with the poor.

Preaching: Two sermons (*khutbah*) will be delivered at the morning celebration. If Eid falls on a Friday, there may be additional sermons at the midday prayer.

Moods: Joy and contentment.

Primary Symbolic Gestures: The men would embrace each other and so would the women, asking God to accept all the virtuous deeds performed in the month.

Restrictions: In Muslim countries, people are not expected to work during the 3 days of Eid-ul Fitr,

Common Customs:

Zakat al-Fitr: A special donation is made on the Eid day. The head of each household calculates the cost of a regular meal times the number of dependents in the household. Either the food or monetary equivalent is given to charity before attending the Eid morning prayer. This donation is in addition to the family's regular Zakat (the annual charitable contribution each Muslim is expected to offer).

Gift Giving: It is common to exchange gifts with one another during Eid.

Visiting: People will visit one another in their homes.

Honoring the Deceased: People often visit the graves of their ancestors or of holy men and women during Eid-ul Fitr.

Fasting/Feasting Practices: This night is one of fast-breaking, a time of feasting!

Additional Worship/Prayer/Ritual Services or Special Focus for Regular Weekly Worship/Prayer:

Communal Prayer: Congregational prayers will take place in the mosque in the morning after sunrise and before the feast.

Prayers for the Deceased: Special prayers are often offered for those who have died.

Six Days of Fasting in Shawwal

Begins/Ends: Since people have already fasted for the entire month of Ramadan, fasting another 6 days in the month of Shawwal (any 6 days) is considered to evoke a particular blessing from God. This fast is entirely optional.

Dhul-Qa'dah (*eleventh month - another holy month where fighting and war is prohibited*) - *means the "month of rest"*

Dhul-Hijjah (*twelfth month - another holy month where fighting and war is prohibited*) - *means "the month of Hajj"*

Hajj – Pilgrimage:

Begins: Many begin their Journey to Mecca during the month of Dhul-Qa'dah even though the required rituals do not begin until the 8th of Dhul-Hijjah.

Ends: Most Pilgrims remain in Mina (a neighborhood of Mecca) until the 13th of Dhul-Hijjah.

Purpose: Fulfills the fifth Pillar of Islam. Making a pilgrimage to Mecca, known as the hajj, is an obligation on all Muslims once in a lifetime if they are physically and financially able to do so without any fear of danger. The pilgrimage commemorates the deep faith of the prophet and patriarch Abraham, his son Ishmael, and his wife Hagar. It also offers the pilgrim the experience of joining with 3 million other Muslims as they stand on the Day of Arafat experiencing the presence and forgiveness of God.

Theological Emphasis: When the pilgrimage is made sincerely, many on hajj will seek forgiveness and aspire for a spiritual rebirth. Those not on pilgrimage will often focus on "faith" – particularly the deep faith of Abraham, Hagar, and Ishmael.

Important Texts: Qur'an, 2:196-200; 5:95-97; and 2:127.

Primary Sites:

Ka'bah: It is an ancient edifice believed to have been built by Abraham and Ishmael as a place of worship to God. Throughout the centuries, however, it ceased to be a place of worship to the one God and instead housed idols of pagan deities. The Prophet Muhammad (PBUH) reclaimed this building and rededicated it to the worship of God alone. Symbolically referred to by the Qu'ran as the "house of God", the Ka'bah sets the direction that Muslims around the world face during the daily prayers. Today the Ka'bah is located in the center of the Grand Mosque in Mecca, Saudi Arabia. It is covered with a richly embroidered cloth and plays a major role in the rituals and symbolic gestures undertaken during the hajj.

Black Stone: A large stone situated in the eastern corner of the Ka'bah. The Prophet Muhammed (PBUH) kissed this stone when he returned to Mecca after his exile in Medina. During the hajj, the pilgrims circumambulate the Ka'bah 7 times and either kiss the Black Stone or point to it as they pass by it each time.

Zamzam Well: After Hagar and Ishmael had been left in the desert by Abraham, they were dying of thirst. It is believed that Ishmael kicked the ground and water sprung forth. The source of the water is called the Zamzam Well and it has never run dry. To accommodate all the people on pilgrimage, the water from the Zamzam Well is now pumped into various sites in the mosque so that the pilgrims can drink from it.

Hilltops of Safa and Marwa: When Hagar was searching for water for herself and her son Ishmael, it is believed that she ran between these two hilltops 7 times. To remember this search and God's saving grace in providing the well of water, pilgrims reenact this search by "running" between the two hilltops. However, because of the large numbers of pilgrims, most will walk rather than run. Multilayered tunnels have been built to accommodate the vast number of pilgrims

Three Stone Pillars: Tradition (from the Qu'ran and Hadith) holds that Satan tempted Abraham, Hagar, and Ishmael to not obey God's command for Abraham to sacrifice his son, Ishmael. The three stone pillars mark the site of each of these temptations. With each temptation, the angel Gabriel told Abraham to pelt Satan with seven stones and with each stoning, Satan disappeared.

The pilgrims repeat this "Stoning of Satan" at the site of each of the three pillars as a symbolic act of drawing closer to God by denouncing Satan and resisting his temptation.

Primary Symbolic Gestures:

Wearing Ihram: "Ihram" refers to both the name of the white two-piece simple clothing that most pilgrims wear during the hajj and the name of the special spiritual state that the pilgrims live in while on pilgrimage. All pilgrims wear sandals and change into the white garb of their ihram at designated stations. The white garb is simply two unhemmed pieces of fabric for the men with one wrapped around the waist and the other draped across one shoulder. Women wear a white hijab that does not cover one's face or hands. Wearing the same type of garb breaks down the differences in culture and economic status among the pilgrims and equalizes everyone. To be in the *spiritual state* of "ihram," one must not shave, wear perfume, have sexual relations, carry weapons, damage plants, swear, quarrel, or perform any dishonest act.

Ritual Purification Rites: Before one embarks on the hajj, one is required to perform a ritual cleansing. At the end of the hajj, in order to symbolize a spiritual new beginning, men either shave or trim their hair and women will cut off a lock of their hair.

Circumambulation of the Ka'bah: Every pilgrim circles the Ka'bah counterclockwise 7 times pointing to the Black Stone with each passing and offering the Takbir Prayer: "There is no god but God, God is the greatest, God is Greatest and to God belongs all praise!" The circumambulation and repetition of the Takbir Prayer joins the diverse group of pilgrims into a unified body. This act creates a sense of harmony among the pilgrims just before the official hajj begins and at the end before everyone goes their separate ways.

Running - Sa'i: Pilgrim "run/walk" 7 times between two hills of Safa and Marwa. Accommodations are made for pilgrims with disabilities.

Stoning Satan: Throwing pebbles/stones at the three stone "pillars" (now walls) is a ritual action denouncing Satan and rejecting temptation. It takes place after the day of Arafat in Mina.

Ritual Animal Sacrifice: God provided an animal to sacrifice instead of Abraham's son, Ishmael. On Eid-ul-Adha (10th of Dhul-Hijjah), sheep, goats, and camels will be sacrificed on behalf of the pilgrims. Muslims not on pilgrimage will also participate in this sacrifice and feast.

Required, Recommended or Optional: Required once in a lifetime of every adult Muslim whose financial situation and health allows.

Restrictions: The Saudi Government usually requires that a woman on pilgrimage be accompanied by one of her close family relatives like her father, husband, or brother.

Fasting/Feasting Practices: Though not required, fasting while on the pilgrimage in Mecca is considered praiseworthy. Those not on the pilgrimage often fast on the 9th of Dhul-Hijjah, the Day of Arafat, in solidarity with those who are making their supplication. *(for Day of Arafat, see below under Pilgrimage Rituals).*

Foods: Meat of the sacrificed animals.

Additional Worship/Prayer/Ritual Services or Special Focus for Regular Weekly Worship/Prayer:

Preparation Prayers:

Rakats: Pilgrims go to the mosque close to the Ka'bah called the Masjid al-Haram and offer two rakats (prayer cycles).

Prayer Ritual: There is a prayer service on the 7th Day of Dhul-Hijjah at the mosque around the Ka'bah.

Pilgrimage Rituals:

8th Day of Dhul-Hijjah: The pilgrims travel to the valley town of Mina which is about 3 miles outside of Mecca where they stay in tents overnight. Many will be in prayer throughout the night preparing their soul for experiencing the presence of the divine the following day.

9th Day of Dhul-Hijjah - Day of Arafat: It is the heart or central focus of the hajj. The pilgrims travel about 9 miles east of Mina to the "Mount of Mercy" or the "Hill of Forgiveness" in the plain of Arafat. It was here that the Prophet Muhammad (PBUH) delivered his farewell sermon. It is on this day that the pilgrims ask for forgiveness, receive mercy from God, and respond anew to God's call on their life. It is believed that on this day, in this place, the veil between heaven and Earth is thinnest and therefore the doors to heaven are opened wide for God to grant forgiveness. There is an expectation that on this day, the pilgrims will encounter the divine presence of God. Three million people stand and contemplate the presence of God and await God's "judgment" on their lives – the gift of forgiveness. The pilgrims experience redemption and emerge as new beings, forgiven and freed to be more faithful and obedient servants of God. From midday until sunset, pilgrims will stand in prayer and supplication. After this Day of Arafat, the pilgrims go halfway back to Mina and spend the night lying on the ground under the open sky in the plain of Muzdalifa. In preparation for the next day, pilgrims gather at least 49 pebbles to take with them to the Stone Pillars in Mina.

10th Day of Dhul-Hijjah: Pilgrims travel the rest of the way to Mina where they throw 7

After the Official Pilgrimage:

Celebration in Mina: Pilgrims continue the celebration of Eid-ul-Adha on the 11th and 12th. People throw 7 pebbles at each of the Stone Pillars/walls on both days. *(see below for the description of Eid-ul-Adha)*

Return to Mecca: Before sunset on the 12th of Dhul-Hijjah, pilgrims return to Mecca.

Circumambulation and Run: Pilgrims may circumambulate the Ka'bah and "run" between the two hilltops again, especially if these acts were not undertaken before the pilgrimage.

Medina: Because the town of Medina played such a crucial role in the life of the Prophet (PBUH) and the history of Islam, many will visit Muhammad's (PBUH) tomb in Medina before returning to their home country.

Eid-ul-Adha – Feast of Sacrifice: *This is the second most important festival in the Islamic year, though it is known as the major Eid.*

Begins: 10th of Zul Hijja (sunset on the 9th).

Ends: After sunset on the 13th of Dhul-Hijjah.

Purpose: Eid-ul-Adha celebrates the redemption that has taken place on the Day of Arafat, the faith of Abraham who was willing to sacrifice his son, Ishmael, and God's provision of an animal as a substitute for Ishmael. On this day, the people make a sacrifice to God. For those on the hajj, Eid-ul-Adha takes place in Mina though Muslims around the world stand in solidarity with those on the hajj and celebrate this 3 day "feast of sacrifice".

Theological Emphasis: Sacrifice. Today, in North America, the emphasis is on sacrificing one's time, money, skills in love for and service to God though the sacrifice of animals is still practiced for those on the hajj and in many parts of the world.

Preaching: A sermon (*khutbah*) will be delivered at the morning celebration. If Eid falls on a Friday, there may be an additional *khutbah* at the midday prayer.

Moods: Joyous!

Common Customs:

Greeting: A common greeting is "Eid Mubarak from our family to yours".

Clothing: It is expected that people will wear their best clothes on this day.

Recitation of *Takbir of Tashriq*: On their way to Eid prayer, people may recite the *Takbir of Tashriq* ("There is no god but God and God is the greatest, God is the greatest and to God belongs all praise.").

Animal Sacrifice: For those Muslim adults who can afford it, it is expected that an animal (sheep, goat, cow) will be sacrificed in remembrance of the gift of the ram that God gave to Abraham as a substitute for the sacrifice of his son. The animal meat is to be divided into 3 parts: one-third is given to those in need, one-third is given away to relatives, and one-third is kept for the family to feast on. Most pilgrims on the hajj will buy a "sacrifice voucher" in Mecca before the Hajj begins. The animal will then be slaughtered in the pilgrim's name on the 10th of Dhul-Hijjah. Some may cook the meat in the tents at Mina for the feast; others will have the meat from their sacrifice packaged and given to charity, even shipped around the world to those in need.

Visitations: It is customary during Eid to visit friends and family in their homes.

Gift Giving: People will exchange gifts with one another.

Honoring the Deceased: It is common to visit the graves of one's ancestors during Eid-ul-Adha and there are special prayers offered for those who have died.

Fasting/Feasting Practices: While people fast before the Eid prayers, feasting will then take place for three days!

Additional Worship/Prayer/Ritual Services or Special Focus for Regular Weekly Worship/Prayer:

Morning Prayer: On the first day of Eid-ul-Adha, after sunrise on the morning of the 10th of Dhul-Hijjah, there will be a time of congregational prayer which will consist of two-cycle prayer followed by two sermons (*khutbah*).

Ghadeer[1] Khumm – Prophet Muhammad's (PBUH) Speech

Begins/Ends: 18th of Dhul-Hijjah

Purpose: Commemorated by the Shias as a festival to mark, according to them, the declaration by Muhammad (PBUH) of Ali as his successor. The Prophet (PBUH) halted at Ghadeer, set up a platform made of saddles, ascended it and delivered a lengthy sermon on his return from the Farewell Pilgrimage at a crossroad before the caravans would part ways and move in different directions. Shias believe that he was commanded by God, based on Qur'an, 5:67, to deliver the message of Ali's succession to the large assembly so that the message would be retained. An excerpt of his message is related by Shaykh Mufid (10th century Shia scholar):

> He [the Prophet (PBUH)] praised and glorified God, and preached most eloquently. He gave the community news of his own death, saying, "I have been summoned, and it is nearly the moment for me to answer. The time has come for me to depart from you. I leave behind me among you two things: if you cleave to them, you will never go astray – that is, the Book of God and my offspring from my family (*ahl al-bayt*)... Then he called out at the top of his voice: 'Am I not more appropriate [as an authority] over you than yourselves:' 'By God, yes!' they answered.

---

[1] Name of an oasis located between Mecca and Medina.

He went on speaking continuously without any interruption and, taking both arms of the Commander of the Faithful [Ali] and raising them so that the white of his armpits could be seen, said, 'Of whomever I am the master (*mawla*), this man, Ali, is his master (*mawla*).'"[1]

Both Sunni and Shia sources attest to the authenticity of this event. The bone of contention surrounds the meaning of the term "mawla." Shias interpret it as "master" with temporal and religious authority whereas the Sunnis take it to mean "friend" with no such authority.

Theological Emphasis: For the Shias, this event underlines that correct and authentic guidance can only be provided by one who is divinely-designated and infallible and, as such, only such a person can establish a just society and correctly interpret the Qur'an.

Preaching: Concept of Imamah (leadership) and succession to the Prophet (PBUH).

Moods: Joyous.

---

[1] Shaykh Mufid, *Kitab al-Irshad* (*The Book of Guidance*), translated by I. K. A. Howard (New York: Tahrike Tarsile Qur'an, 1981), 124.

Comparisons and Conclusions

The yearly ritual calendars of Jews, Christians, and Muslims are extremely diverse and yet each of the Abrahamic traditions remembers, commemorates, observes, and re-enacts the formative textual and historical narratives that are at the heart of the religion.
Active participation in the various observances keeps adherents rooted in the people and events that have shaped who each has come to be, as individuals and as a religious community.

Forming community is a result of a group gathering for prayer, worship, and ritual observance. It is not necessarily knowing the reasons, history, or theological significance of participating in the particular religious practices associated with each observance that is essential (although this knowledge can provide a deeper experience). For many practitioners, it is engaging in these practices collectively that builds social bonds and forms community. It is the Jewish community or Christian community or Muslim community that provides the foundation for relationships that sustain individuals and entire populations during times of struggle and times of joy. The social value of community formation as a purpose or by-product of ritual observance cannot be overstated.

Participating in ritual observances re-situates us within the community of faith, reiterates the story that provides a foundation for meaning in our lives, and offers us opportunities to encounter the mystery of the divine. Taken as a whole, the yearly observances proclaim a God, the God of Abraham, who calls us into relationship and formed people in different times and places to be a community to support one another in their faithfulness to God, their care for one another, and their relations with those outside the community. God is portrayed as one who offers mercy and forgiveness, love and second chances. But God also sets up high expectations for us by calling us to acknowledge our sins and shortcomings, seek forgiveness, live an ethic of compassion, resist temptation, refocus our priorities, and choose life in God.

Comparisons

In learning about the various yearly observances and practices of these "siblings in faith" (Judaism, Christianity, Islam), there were multiple "aha" moments as we found common themes and practices. It was also striking when two of the religious traditions shared something in common but not the third one. For example, Jews and Muslims have clearly designated occasions for celebrating the revelation from God that forms the textual basis for their religion (Shavuot for Jews – the giving of the Torah by God to Moses and the Hebrew people, Ramadan for Muslims – one aspect celebrates the revelation of the Qu'ran to Mohammed [PBUH]). Christianity doesn't have a day or season or occasion that celebrates the revelation of any sacred text and yet Jesus is called the "Logos," the "Word" of God as well as "Emmanuel" (God with us).

Each of the Abrahamic religions includes in their yearly calendar times for looking inward to one's spiritual shortcomings and other times for reaching out in gift giving and offering charity, times for mourning violence and the sins we commit against God and one another, as well as times of great joy and celebration recognizing God's gracious mercy.

Below is a list of comparisons ordered alphabetically by topic:

Affirmations of Faith:

Judaism:

Shema

Hear O Israel, the Lord is our God, the Lord is One. Blessed is the name of His Glorious Majesty forever and ever.

Christianity:

Apostle's Creed

I believe in God the Father Almighty, maker of heaven and earth;

And in Jesus Christ, God's only son, our Lord: who was conceived of the Virgin Mary, suffered under Pontius Pilate, was crucified, died, and was buried. He descended into hell. The third day he rose from the dead; he ascended into heaven, and sits at the right hand of God, the Father Almighty; from thence he shall come to judge the quick (living) and the dead.

I believe in the Holy Spirit,
the holy catholic[1] church,
the communion of saints,
the forgiveness of sins,
the resurrection of the body,
and the life everlasting.

Or

---

[1] "catholic" (lower case "c") means "universal".

Nicene Creed

We believe in one God, the Father, the Almighty,
maker of heaven and earth, of all that is, seen and
unseen.

We believe in one Lord, Jesus Christ, the only Son
of God, eternally begotten of the Father, God from
God, Light from Light, true God from true God,
begotten, not made, of one Being with the Father;
through him all things were made.
For us and for our salvation
he came down from heaven,
was incarnate of the Holy Spirit and the Virgin
Mary
and became truly human.
For our sake he was crucified under Pontius Pilate;
he suffered death and was buried.
On the third day he rose again in accordance with
the scriptures;
He ascended into heaven and is seated at the right
hand of the Father.
He will come again in glory to judge the living and
the dead, and his kingdom
will have no end.

We believe in the Holy Spirit, the Lord, the giver of life,
who proceeds from the Father and the Son,
who with the Father and the Son is worshiped and
glorified,
who has spoken through the prophets.

We believe in the one holy catholic and apostolic church.
We acknowledge one baptism for the forgiveness of sins.
We look for the resurrection of the dead, and the life of
the world to come.

Islam:

Shahadah
I testify that there is no god but God and I testify that
Muhammad (pbuh) is His servant and Messenger

Birth as a Religious Community:
    Judaism: Shavuot
    Christianity: Pentecost
    Islam: Hijra

Daily Prayer:
    Judaism: Shaharit – morning
                Minha - afternoon
                Maariv - evening
    Christianity: Matins – dawn (about 6 am)
                        Terce – mid-morning (about 9 am)
                        Sext – noontime
                        None – mid-afternoon (about 3 pm)
                        Vespers – evening - sunset
                        Compline – before bed
    Islam: Fajr – pre-dawn (at least 10-15 minutes
                before sunrise)
            Dhuhr – midday but before Asr
            'Asr – late afternoon
            Maghrib – after sunset but before dusk
            'Isha – evening (after dusk)[1]

---

[1] Shias generally combine Dhuhr and 'Asr prayers in one sitting and Maghrib and 'Isha although it is preferable but not mandatory in their school of thought to separate the prayers. As such, the valid time for Dhuhr and 'Asr starts at midday and ends at sunset. Likewise, the timing for Maghrib and 'Isha starts 15 minutes after sunset and ends at mid-point of the night.

Day of Atonement/Day of Redemption:
    Judaism: Yom Kippur
    Christians: Good Friday/Easter Sunday
    Muslims: Day of Arafat during the Hajj pilgrimage

Everyday Visible Adornments that Identify an Adherent of
a Particular Religion:
    Judaism: Kippa and other head coverings, Star of
        David necklace, Tzitzit (for Orthodox Jews)
    Christianity: Cross necklace, cross tattoo
    Islam: Hijab for many women; beard for some men

Festival of Light:
    Judaism: Hanukkah
    Christianity: Advent

Future Redemptive Figures:
    Judaism: Looks toward the coming of the Messiah
        (or Messianic Age)
    Christianity: looks toward the second coming of
        Jesus (or the realized Kingdom of God)
    Islam: Shia Muslims look toward the reappearance
        of their Twelfth Imam (the Mahdi, The
        Guided One) who was born in the ninth
        century along with Jesus Christ. Sunni
        Muslims believe that the Mahdi is yet to be
        born.

Major Fasts:
    Judaism: Yom Kippur and Tisha B'Av (fasting from
        sunset to sunset)
    Christianity: Season of Lent (fasting in a way that
        giving up all food or particular foods would
        be considered sacrificial)

Islam: Month of Ramadan (fasting from sunrise to sunset)

Major Times of Self-inventory:
Judaism: The month of Elul in preparation for Rosh ha-Shanah and Yom Kippur and the 10 Days of Awe that are bracketed by these two holy days.
Christianity: Season of Lent
Islam: The Nights of Qadr

Moods:
Most Joyous:
Judaism: Sukkot and Simchat Torah
Christianity: Christmas and Easter
Islam: Eid-ul Fitr and Eid-ul Adha and the Prophet's birthday[1]

Most solemn:
Judaism: Yom Kippur and Tisha B'Av
Christianity: Holy Week, especially Good Friday
Islam: The Nights of Qadr[2]

Most frivolous:
Judaism: Purim
Christianity: Shrove Tuesday/Mardi Gras/Carnival

New Year:
Judaism: New Year for months – 1st of Nissan
New Year for animal tithing – 1st of Elul

---

[1] For Shia Muslims, in addition to the Prophet, they commemorate the birthday of the Twelfth Imam.
[2] For Shia Muslms, Ashura is also viewed as solemn.

New Year for years – Rosh Hashanah (1st of Tishrei);

New Year for trees – Tu B'Shevat (15th of Shavat)

Christianity: First Sunday of Advent

Islam: Hijrah

Prayer Postures;

Judaism: Shuckling (rocking motion); bowing; sitting and standing

Christianity: Hands folded or in "prayer position" with head bowed; kneeling; standing in orans position (arms raised up), sitting.

Islam: Salat prayer that includes positions for hands and body during times of standing, bowing, prostration, and sitting.

Prayer/Worship Space:

Judaism: Ark – facing Jerusalem

Christianity: Altar/table – originally on the east wall because biblical texts imply that Jesus' second coming will be from the east.

Islam: Minbar - facing Mecca

Pulpit:

Judaism: The *bimah* (from *bamah*, meaning "high place") is a raised platform with a reading desk from which the Torah, Prophets, and Five Scrolls are chanted. In many communities, the entire service is conducted from the platform.

Christianity: The pulpit is a lectern style piece of furniture from which the sermon is delivered. While usually located on a raised area called the "chancel," the pulpit may or may not be additionally elevated. The pulpit is often considered a place of authority by which the priest/pastor (in some traditions a lay person) interprets sacred texts for the community; a place of mediation between humanity and the divine.

Islam: A staircase-like structure from where the sermon/khutbah is delivered.

Remembering the Deceased:

Judaism: Yizkor services (Yom Kippur and the three major pilgrimage festivals at the end of each), Yom ha-Shoah, Yom ha-Zikaron, Yahrzeit for individuals

Christianity: All Saints Day, All Souls Day

Islam: Ashura for Shia Muslims

Revelation:

Judaism: Shavuot

Christianity: Christmas. Jesus is considered to be the "Word" ("logos") of God. Jesus' life is the revelation of God.

Islam: Bi'thath – the beginning of the Prophet's mission in 610 when he received the first five verses of the Qur'an (96:1-5)

Ritual Acts that Connect One Observance to Another:

Judaism: The lulav (palm branch) used in the ritual of the four species in Sukkot will sometimes be used to light the fire that will destroy the leaven for the following year's Pesach preparations.

Christianity: The palm leaves used in the Palm Sunday procession will be burned and the ashes will be used for the following year's Ash Wednesday service.

Textual Revelation:
> Judaism: Shavuot. Moses received the commandments from G-d.
> Islam: Lailatul Qadr. The essence of the Qur'an was revealed on Laylatul Qadr and its elaboration was subsequently transmitted to the Prophet Muhammad (PBUH) over a course of twenty-three years.

Times of Rest:
> Judaism: Shabbat (sunset Friday to sunset Saturday)
> Christianity: Sunday
> Islam: Friday

Times of Seeking Forgiveness:
> Judaism: Days of Awe
> Christianity: Season of Lent
> Islam: Five daily prayers and Ramadan

Times of Thanksgiving:
> Judaism: Sukkot
> Christianity: Whenever the Eucharist/Holy Communion/Lord's Supper is celebrated. Eucharist means to give thanks

White Ritual Garb for Laity:
> Judaism: White kittel worn by men in relationship to death and at other sacred times. Women may also wear white garments on certain holy days.
> Christianity: White baptismal garment
> Islam: White Ihram worn during the hajj pilgrimage

Conclusion

Each religious tradition has a rich array of observances and practices as they journey through the various rhythms of their year. There are tremendous differences between us and amazing points of commonality. Learning about the yearly practices of other religious traditions has the potential to deepen our own religious practices while we also gain an understanding and appreciation for the rich practices held by others.

Since beginning this project in 2014, much has changed in our world in relationship to immigrants and the religious beliefs and practices they bring with them to the United States. Islamaphobia, hateful speech and violent acts toward "the other" are on the rise. It is the sincere hope of all involved in this book that people, especially students training to be religious leaders, will get to know persons from other religions and learn about the practices, as well as the beliefs, that sustain their faith. It is important that religious leaders collaborate in communities to diffuse hate and violence and contribute to solutions to poverty and homelessness so that we can create a more peace-filled environment for ourselves and future generations. May this book be a small step toward that end.

Made in the USA
Las Vegas, NV
07 December 2021

36469325R00098